CONFESSIONS AND TESTIMONY OF A

Christian Prisoner

Bring comfort, light, and direction to all prisoners of the state or of addiction and/or those looming sins, which according to God's Holy Word, most certainly include us all.

RAY AMATO

ISBN 978-1-0980-5884-5 (paperback)
ISBN 978-1-0980-5885-2 (digital)

Christian Faith Publishing, Inc.
832 Park Avenue
Meadville, PA 16335
www.christianfaithpublishing.com

All scriptures taken from NKJV.

Printed in the United States of America

Contents

Poetry and Proverbial Section

ACKNOWLEDGMENTS

I have so many friends and family members to thank for the encouragement that led to this work, including my wife, Anne, who I married this year on Valentine's Day. However, the greatest encouragement came from my late father, Raymond G. Amato, who back in the early days, would patiently listen to me read my papers. He was amazed at how far I had come since I struggled so much as a child with all English-related subjects in school. He made me believe I could be a writer if I kept at it. Now on the doorstep of sixty years comes my first book. Thanks, Dad. See you in heaven. How's the golf course up there? Thanks too to my mother, Patricia, and my late stepfather, Marco Hernandez, who funded the book. God bless you all.

Poets Seek "The Answer"

Well beyond the "Age of Reason," it had become the mid-twentieth century. The atheist and agnostic philosophers had spoken, the psychiatrists had written their books, and so too had Mr. Charles Darwin; basically concurring that God is dead! These infamous men of letters have for more than a century conducted scholasticism along confused roads to destination meaningless—fading to barren in hope as faith and frankly logic had been taken for long meandering strolls in dark places. Consequently, with no divine absolutes, the guiding light of conscience became dim and callous receding ever more progressively in the western world. Even that "American Woman"[1]/ Lady Liberty came under fire as her freedom was found wanting and her hope waning; "do this, don't do that" there began to be "Signs"[2] everywhere, then adding insult to injury, a seething materialism quite naturally arose, generating a whirlpool that pulls steadily down. It was subtle, though, you know, "Kind of a Drag."[3]

Baby boomers born to that great and gallant generation now in adolescence felt lost. In attempt to fill the void

---

[1]   The Guess Who.
[2]   Fine Man Electrical Band.
[3]   J. Holvay—The Buckinghams.

the blues, jazz, folk, and rock 'n' roll poets of the sixties and seventies endeavor to aid the "Mod" or "Now Generation" in finding meaning and direction as the unprepared Church had largely dropped the ball. Enter stage right the rebellious beatniks of the 1950s who yield to the hippies of the turbulent 1960s full of youthful energy, but naturally with the usual lack of experience. As though prophets the Fabulous Four begged, "Nowhere Man[4] please listen." One could easily sense by this generation's art a youthful and hopeful vibrance, but it swiftly shifted to protest in heated rebellion against the war in Southeast Asia and against a rising police state, like a Kent State—"Four dead in O-HI-O."[5] Still, hope stirred deep down as the Church wakes from her slumber. Enter the likes of Billy Graham, John MacArthur, Chuck Smith, and so many more leading the way to revival with open minds and open doors at the chapels. We also respectfully remember Dr. King's movement and martyrdom. Such people of faith have always known "The Answer,"[6] that it was accomplished at Calvary some two thousand years ago and has since been proclaimed from the rooftops, but a minority of blind guides have somehow "slashed the Pearly Gates"[7] for so many, or else, they slammed them in their faces. Thankfully, no man or devil can shut what our Creator has opened.

---

4   J. Lennon, P. McCartney—Beatles.
5   Neil Young—C,S,N,Y.
6   Justin Hayward—The Moody Blues.
7   N. Young—Song Title: Thrasher.

It all began in relative innocence as the left coast kids went "California Dreamin'"[8] and "Surfin' USA,"[9] the Grateful Dead sang of that famed Christian martyr "Saint Stephen[10] with a Rose," and make no mistake, it was that distant Rose of Sharon, which they had in mind, that now publicly forbidden Lilly of the Valley. On the east coast, folk singers strum protest songs in the Village and at New Port. As President Johnson escalates the war in Vietnam, someone cries, "The pigs of ruthless progress love their futile lords." Elvis telegraphs yet another plight: "Another poor baby child is born in the Ghetto."[11] The kind or perhaps not-so-kind intentions of the welfare state backfires in a dismal tailspin, as nationwide riots blaze in the ghetto night, in Central Park poets pray, "A bridge over troubled waters"[12] while young rockers inspired by the blues movement out of the Mississippi delta ring out from the Old Lion at London's Royal Albert Hall and from the Young Lion at New York's Madison Square Garden, Shea Stadium, and from Yasgur's Farm, "Like a butterfly over the nation" the song was called "Woodstock"[13] and so too was the festival in the summer of '69, the summer of those amazing Mets, the winter of Joe Willy and the Jets, and the first lunar landing.

Ricky Nelson wondered, should he go to a "Garden Party"[14] and mix with some old friends? Should he try his

---

[8] The Mamas and the Papas.
[9] B. Wilson, C. Berry—song by Beach Boys.
[10] Lesh, Hunter, Garcia—Greatful Dead.
[11] Mac Davis, performed also by Elvis Presley.
[12] Simon to Garfunkel.
[13] Joni Mitchell, performed Crosby, Stills, Nash.
[14] Ricky Nelson.

luck? "If memories were all I sang," he said, "I'd rather drive a truck." Forgive this historic venture, but both I'd suggest should be preferred to a foolish war; nevertheless, all three should be preferred to fleeing the glory of "Protocol,"[15] which is heartlessness in more ways than one, above all dishonorable. In any event, turns out one may still become the forty-second president of the United States in this new and confused utopia. From the British Isles, the kids cry out for their beloved countryman, "They're all wasted."[16] Back in the States, in attempt to give credence to revival, a question was put forth: "Have you ever seen the rain coming down on a sunny day?"[17] For to be sure, "The sunshine they'd been waiting for had turned to rain"[18]: very hot rain; tracers, mortars, rockets, and napalm, oh yea and Agent Orange too.

Out of the City of Angels, a new dimension of soulish singer rose "Up Up and Away"[19] in their beautiful balloon, almost prophesying, ever hoping that the "Age of Aquarius"[20] soon would dawn, but it did not as hope for peace and unity proved spurious, a fleeing dream deferred. Those professors so long ago had predicted an evolution of mankind upward to utopia yet humanity is growing less and less humane on an ever steep decline. Yep, truth is, more people were killed in the twentieth century than in the prior nineteen centuries in aggregate counting from the

---

[15] Gordon Lightfoot.
[16] P. Townshed, song Baba O'Riley, The Who.
[17] J. Fogerty, C.C.R.
[18] J. Hayward, song—The Story in Your Eyes, by Moody Blues.
[19] J Webb, performed by The 5th Dimension.
[20] J. Rado/G. Ragni, performed by The 5th Dimension.

dawn of Christendom. On time, as well as in time, Mr. Bob Zimmerman had in his usual way suggested in that vague yet clarion cadence of a poet, "The answer, my friend, is blowin' in the wind"[21] and I would add, like the Holy Spirit at Pentecost. But those pedantic professors refuse to allow for such "Superstition"[22]; therefore, they are no better at deciphering spiritual matters than is a blind man seeking for a black cat in a dark room, they cannot discover The Answer even as they forever stand "on the threshold of a dream."[23]

That great debacle, that foolish fiasco, that police action, that dragging wasteful war of attrition in Vietnam was finally after more than a decade brought to an end in demoralizing failure (the first war our country had in its entire history lost) under the tenure of Tricky Dick Nixon, who perhaps was not as bad as people made out; nevertheless, "he had a few of his own bills to pay."[24] However, the chiefs did not dismantle the war machine; rather, they renovated it for another day. In place of hot fire came cold war, "20th Century Man's"[25] hydrogen bombs and biological warfare. Instead of feeding her children, their inheritance the Lady fleeced them, feeding instead the machine absurd fortunes, an admitted obligatory obscenity in the face of numerous opposing, and we might add, imposing tyrannical regimes. Apparently in this post Age of Reason, lording

---

[21] Bob Dylan.
[22] Steve Wonder.
[23] The Moody Blues.
[24] David Bowie, lyrics from song "Young Americans."
[25] Ray Davies—The Kinks.

over others has become ever more in vogue throughout this utopian world of modernity.

Many a disenchanted youth of those, so-called, counterculture days who having had failed to bring about positive change during their restless years morph into the preppies and yuppies of the eighties and nineties, settling for false security and affluence, a miserable business of accepting a spiritually bleak universe—the only kind of universe, incidentally, that academia had offered. They sought adventure in their elders imagined safe haven, ironically in an escalating atomic age where peace is brokered by threat of annihilation, where ceasefires are merely an interlude for reloading and where the practice of ghoulish genocide is called ethnic cleansing or even more evil perhaps, population control (in a world of vast fertile fields and forests on a garden planet). The rest, those who yet refused to yield to these blind guides, had foolishly attempted to escape via psychedelic trips all across this land, some even "Shuffled off to Buffalo," "Truckin'"[26] in that Timothy Leary fashion. Others chased dragons in barren deserts upon "A Horse With No Name"[27] though some called the lady a heroine. Apparently, Mr. Young had spoken from experience when he wrote, "I've seen the needle and the damage done, a little part of it in everyone and every junky is like a setting sun,"[28] so too had those street survivors warned of "That

---

[26] Hunter, Grateful Dead.
[27] D. Bunnell—America.
[28] Neil Young.

Smell,[29] that smell of death all around," "One toke over the line."[30]

Staggered in the throes of alcohol addiction, some groped excessively that pagan god Bacchus, others indulged John Barleycorn or various distilled spirits seeking a life in some spirit any old way. They ran hard and long for illusive pleasures in blinding snowstorms, a bewitching numbing extravagance. Uppers, downers, from slow to fast to too fast, from palaces they fell to prisons they crashed. In the peculiar solace of their cells of asylum entered a soft clear light which the quiet and careful could perceive. Some became Jesus Freaks, others not as obvious, yet still caught in this confounded web of addiction many stumbled and tumbled for years to come. In spite of good intentions, a lifetime of smoke and mirrors (literal or otherwise) continue to disappoint as character defects prove a tiresome and arduous "Long Strange Trip." Always in the mix, however, was a universal beauty which they did not fail to notice, like a "Starry Starry Night"[31] or a "Rocky Mountain High"[32] or visions of that morning sun rising like a "Red Rubber Ball,"[33] or "Like The Rain The Park And Other Things,"[34] and how about those barefooted flower girls.

Finally, that poetic book of verse perfect in its mastery of love and knowledge came into focus stating truisms proved right in the course of time as a crown of gray hair

---

[29] VanZant/Collins performed by Lynyrd Skynyrd.
[30] M Brewer performed by Brewer & Shipley.
[31] Don Mclean, song title "Vincent."
[32] J. Denver, Mike Taylor.
[33] Woodley, Simon performed by "The Cyrkle."
[34] Duboff, Kornfeld performed by "The Cowsills."

is by grace granted to those who in defiance of the nay-sayers would not give up their clumsy quest for truth and meaning. Now hopefully "We Won't Get Fooled Again"[35] as we come nearer to the point of understanding, finally becoming hip to the fact that "all things" (whether in the palace or the prison) "work together for the good to those who love God, to those who are the called according to his purpose" (Romans 8:28). It has become manifest that those who through patience in long suffering would not disown God on the word of men or demons, God in turn will neither disown, "A bruised reed He will not break" (Isaiah 42:3). Truth is, God is the source of all. He is the epitome of that very cool and kind peace with justice for all, which we had sought. He is beyond the range of the wise in their own eyes, but revealed especially to the lost and mislead children, to the un-beautiful, and to those severely judged ones, to those who now call Him the only wise One who is full of patience and forgiveness, He is also called Love, which is of course "The Answer" we poets at heart have for so long sought and often spoke of, but by now are beginning to understand. As it is written so will it be, "and He will wipe away every tear from their eyes" (Revelation 7:17).

Well then, that is in part how I perceive the unique life and times of "My Generation"[36] as we proceed through time and space, tumbling toward that so illusive and long-awaited true utopia under the leadership of a perfectly good and wise King. Come when you will, "Jesus Christ

---

[35] Pete Townshend/The Who.
[36] P. Townshend/The Who.

Superstar."[37] Love, peace, tolerance, and forgiveness sprinkled with faith equals "The Answer."

Forgive me now if I digress, but I must say, "If there's a rock 'n' roll heaven,[38] then you know they've got a hell of a band." Who knows, they might be playing "My Sweet Lord"[39] just now and critics will undoubtedly say, "Mr. Harrison has never sounded better."

---

[37] Tim Rice (song performed in the Broadway musical of the same name).

[38] Alan O'Day, performed by "The Righteous Brothers."

[39] George Harrison.

THREE DANGERS IN CHRISTENDOM

1. Judging oneself too harshly.

The more progress we make in our Christian walk, the better we come to know God, the closer we become with God, the more sensitive we become to our sins, even in the case of their decrease. The danger is we may judge ourselves so harshly that we question if we are real. This is not all in vain, however, because it is God's way of drawing us back home, but we shouldn't be too hard on ourselves since it can, if taken too far, be unproductive and discouraging. Balance at this point is deciphered from the holy scriptures and enhanced the more in spiritual prayer and meditation on those scriptures, for as Jesus had said, "God is Spirit and those who worship Him must worship in spirit and truth" (John 4:24).

The devil's name "Satan" means accuser and adversary, but God is our forgiving Father and advocate. Sensitivity to sin is built in for the good of the child of God, but again, we must continually forgive ourselves; otherwise we find disagreement with God, the One who is ultimately the offended party of all our sins yet the perfect forgiver, removing our sins from us as far as the east is from the west. Overwhelming self-condemnation may disguise itself as humility, while in reality prove itself a detriment, causing us to become discouraged just when courage is what we are most in need of as Christian soldiers commissioned to serve under the King of kings who no longer rides on a lowly donkey, but now on a high white charger.

2. Considering others' undue judgment against us.

There is a different yet similar danger when we sin. When we sin (which we will and we do), our adversary and his demonic agents may, by rights, granted them bring human accusers and tormentors against us so to heighten the consequences of our wayward ventures, exasperating our guilt and personal disappointment, which may feel all too real. This can be a very demoralizing thing, even though to an extent a true thing, but again, it can be deceptive and damaging, given to much leverage. Damaged and weakened; things are made the worse as we appear powerless and as mere actors in full view of the world, a world where we are God's ambassadors. As we recall these incidences, we remember severe injury to our mental and spiritual wellbeing, quite the opposite of those times when we find harmony with God, and far more severely than our unspiritual fellows' experience, for the Lord disciplines His own. God has given us free will, so when we choose to transgress Him against His good advice (to which we are privy) the devil and his host have us dead to rights. Thankfully, even what the devils' intent for evil, God uses for our eventual good, but this way is hard. These are some of the deceptive tricks of dark forces that can reduce us to loss and sorrow, but even here a true Christian remains safety saved even if narrowly, even if only like a man escaping a house on fire, but we strive for better things, even God's desire to bless us rather than to discipline.

3. Maintaining an unforgiving spirit toward others.

There is yet a worse danger in Christendom, perhaps the worst danger; it is unforgiveness toward others. It is most dangerous of all because carried too far, it may disqualify us as true believers in our risen Lord. Perhaps you think I take too much liberty here, so I will quote Jesus from Matthew 6:14–15, where He plainly says, "For if you forgive men their trespasses, your heavenly Father will also forgive you, but if you do not forgive men their trespasses, neither will your Father forgive your trespasses." Friends, the scriptures plainly say, that if we be not forgiven, we will not be permitted in God's presence, and God resides where He presides in heaven, but Satan our accuser resides in hell, and it seems so will those who follow his ways. I mean, those who are accusers, rather than forgivers. That's how it reads, and that's how it feels in spirit and so it's fair to conclude that that's how it is, or at least, how God wants us to understand it, and that's good enough for me.

In conclusion, I say to myself first, pray often in the Spirit and God will make us understand that we are completely forgiven—continually, that we belong to Him, at which point forgiving others and ourselves comes naturally, as well as continual growth in life. Here the knowledge imparted says Jesus the Good Shepherd is irrevocably our Shepherd. Again, we go to the scriptures for conformation, Jesus is the speaker:

> "This is the will of the Father who sent Me, that of all He has given Me I should lose nothing, but should raise it up at the last day." (John 6:39)

Ocean County Jail, 2013
Toms River, NJ

PURSUING OUR TRIUNE GOD
Essay 1

In the spirit of St. Thomas Aquinas (1225–1274) who in his youth boldly asked, "What is God?" we also ask. A mystic of the high Middle Ages, Thomas was a forerunner of the "Reformation," as well as the "Renaissance," a philosopher and a pioneer who sought God in history, mathematics, the natural sciences, and of course theologically. His prolific writing reveals God's faithful reward to all who diligently seek Him—as "Wise Men" always have. Not only did Thomas's writings reveal God to his readers and hearers, but most emphatically, his chaste character revealed God. In fact, on his death bed at age forty-nine, he asked to have his confession heard, and I'll quote Mr. Chesterton from his book titled *St. Thomas Aquinas*. Listen to the thoughts and words of Thomas's attending fellows, as Chesterton so eloquently tells it.

> "In the world of that mind (St. Thomas) there was a wheel of angels, and a wheel of planets, and a wheel of plants or of animals; but there was also a just and intelligible order of all earthly things, a sane authority and a self-respecting liberty, and

a hundred answers to a hundred questions in the complexity of ethics or economics. But there must have been a moment, when men knew that, that thunderous mill of thought had stopped suddenly; and that after the shock of stillness that wheel would shake the world no more; that there was nothing now within that hollow house but a great hill of clay; and the confessor, who had been with him in the inner chamber, ran forth as if in fear, and whispered that, "his confession had been that of a child of five." (G. K. Chesterton)

Unquestionably, Aquinas knew a boatload about God, but more importantly he knew God.

A debilitating confusion on that subject "What is God" has continually ebbed and flowed since the birth of the Church, or since the dawn of man for that matter. In the beginning, the Church's relationship with God was most potent and pure due to the cleansing effect of persecution from without, which always sorts out the murky and polluting effects of pretenders. It became cloudy and corrupted generally starting in the fourth century AD when the church became somewhat forcibly "universalized," legalized, and politicized, which ironically coincides with the world's descent into "The Dark Ages." Please note, it was not the church dragging the world down as critics like to suggest, but it was really the infiltration of the world into the Church, compromising the Church that dragged both down. Point is, the purifying, seasoning, and persevering effect of the church, like the salt of the earth, when it loses its savor it drops noticeably in worth and usefulness.

In the "Middle Ages," the likes of Saint Thomas Aquinas, Dominic, Bonaventure, the great professor Albertus Magnus, and many others struggled against these powers to correct this malady. In succession, the reformers Wycliffe, Hus, Luther, Zwingly, Calvin, and Knox and many others made their heroic contributions: directing common folks of faith along this arduous trek of more fully knowing God—arduous, I say because of its evil interruptions, not its delightful procession or ends. Since the nineteenth century during the "Age of Enlightenment," some fields of science, especially those dealing with the theory of evolution, along with atheistic philosophers and liberal theologians, have set us back once again bringing doubt to God's true Word. Now we must fight our way through again, retaking the ground our forefathers had gained. Our foe is the same—that same, "father of lies," Lucifer. "How you are fallen from heaven, O Lucifer, son of the morning! How you are cut down to the ground, you who weakened the nations!" (Isaiah 14:12).

To know God should be of paramount importance, an urgent practicality for mankind, who was specifically created by God, in His own image, for fellowship with Himself. God is diversity in unity. When we speak of our triune God—Father, Son, Holy Spirit—the three persons or personalities of God, who are ONE, it always seems to sound somewhat mechanical and contrived. This is because we are trying to understand an entity of infinite power and knowledge, who exists everywhere in time and space, as well as in another eternal dimension in a strictly spirit state (with the exception of Jesus the God-Man since His incarnation in Bethlehem). The way from the mechanical to a more natural and fluent apprehension of God is through seeking in faith, which is then by grace granted, in a growing awareness of spirituality discerned truths as faith matures.

WHAT IS GOD?

The Bible says and so is understood and explained with complete unity among all true denominations of the Church through their duly established doctrinal writings and professions of faith to be saying that God is a Trinity—meaning, He is three persons or three personalities who comprise the One true and eternal creator God. But why must God be a plurality? I suppose the answers to this question may be so wide and deep as to be utterly unfathomable humanly speaking; in fact I'm sure of it. But I think we can state one reason with fair confidence and it is simply this: The Bible plainly tells us that "God is love" (1 John 4:16). But to express one's love, one would need an object to love. And since God is eternal in the past, as well as in the future, He predates His creation of all physical things, including mankind. Therefore, by necessity He would have need of another person or personality so to exercise His most glowing attribute, LOVE. Point is, Christ always was, listen to the inter-trinitarian conversation long before Jesus's birth. "Come let US go down and there confuse their language, that they may not understand one another's speech" (Gen. 11:7) or even before the creation of mankind, "Let us make man in our image" (Gen. 1:26). The point is, God is a perfectly united eternal plurality who is one.

> "In the beginning was the WORD,
> and the WORD was with God,
> and the WORD was God. He was
> in the beginning with God.
> All things were made through Him,
> and without Him nothing was
> made that was made." (John 1:1–3, by
> the "WORD" is meant Christ)

Secondly, we should remember that God by definition must be all in all; above all and over all, therefore the persons of God must be equal in essence within the God head. But in three persons, we find three unique relationships in function manifested. Probably, it is our limited intellect and our limitations in language and experience that this word picture is offered, as it admittedly is vague and nebulous, that is, mysterious. The Holy Scriptures suggest that God functions in the Trinity as Father, Son, and Holy Spirit. This affords us a basic familiarity apparent in natural life.

God the Father represents the Fatherhood of all things, from our environment (the universe), to our life and sustenance, to our eternal souls; the Father is Providence. The highest honor is due to Him, which Jesus had so perfectly demonstrated. Ideally speaking, this should be familiar to us by our terrestrial relationships with our biological fathers.

One note, however, when we honor any of the three persons of God, we honor all equality, since they are, after all, ONE! Behold the mystery.

Jesus Christ the Son pictures to us, the Good King, brotherhood, and friendship. Such a thorough brother and friend, as to taste death with us, and defeat death for us, making possible an eternal relationship between the Father and us under His Sovereign Kingship—that is, Lordship, for if He is not one's Lord. The danger is, He also may not be one's Savior, understand we are not talking about perfection, but rather progress; remember God is love and love is hopeful and fair, and also remember, He wants very much to receive us as sons and daughters, this also is the "Good News." Anyway, among the Godhead, the Son can be most readily related to because of His humanity!

Then back we go to the complete abstract again in the person of the Holy Spirit, He who represents our present help, bridging communion with the Father and the Son, this owing to the fact that He is the outreach of them who are seated in the Throne Room of the Kingdom, so to speak, for we need to understand these are word pictures as the Bible relates them. The Holy Spirit is our counselor and comforter, enabling us to better know our loving and providential Father, He assures us also that our King is a very good, kind, and generous Shepherd, the Holy Spirit resident in us is the guarantee of our salvation so that we may truly know that we know!

Truth is, men by their explanations can at best only chip off fleeting sparks, as to explain our Triune God. It is God alone who can turn the light on, and when the light is on, one can see Him since He is The Light. Listen to the Apostle: "This is the message which we have heard from Him and declare to you, that God is light and in Him is no darkness at all" (1 John 1:5). The concept of the Holy Trinity, however, is ultimately inexplicable in this dispensation, even for men such as St. Thomas, St. Augustine, the Holy Apostles, the Church Fathers and Elders, down through the Church age. The Holy Trinity was even more opaque to the Old Testament saints, such as Abraham (our father of faith) or Moses (a shadow of Christ, in that he delivered Israel out of bondage) or even King David who was Jesus's progenitor on Mary's side. Not since the Garden of Eden has any man enjoyed unimpeded knowledge of or communion with God (except of course Jesus the God-Man). After the "Fall" of man, and by extension the Fall of all creation, brought about by the willful sin of Adam, that intimate communion was gravely veiled, and this veil continues to this day, though through faith in Christ and growing obedience we find rents in the veil so to speak.

Obedience to God is faith, and the condition under which the Holy Spirit proliferates the process of sanctification through the miracle of the "New Birth," bringing an ever-clearer vision of God, as well as a certainty that He is, and that we will eternally be with Him—at which point, even death holds no terror. Our best examples are the countless martyrs who faithfully faced prisons and death over simply renouncing Christ. Such faith is available to us all, but a complete restoration of the Garden experience will have to wait until we are finally clothed in our new, imperishable, glorified bodies.

So again, complete understanding will continue to elude us in part, and that must be by God's design for His own good reasons, but we are encouraged by God's ongoing invitation to a growing relationship with Him, for both His joy and ours. Speaking of my own case, far too often, the colossal benefit such a pursuit in study and prayer would bring about, gets treated with mundane or casual interest. Little interest makes for little effort, which of course yields little benefit, and a fickle and fleeting hope. We have been given a spirit of free will and high intellect, and God has offered an ongoing invitation, but He will not force Himself on anyone for eternity who has his life long refused Him. He is God after all; He has done His work in creation and redemption, now it is ours to acknowledge and accept Him, according to knowledge, which again is found in the Holy Scriptures and is by the Holy Spirit unveiled (mainly it seems during prayer or in meditation, similar things).

Simply stated, God can be progressively better known if He is by us sought. Something I believe a joy and a privilege certainty never a burden. If, however, we continue to be content to know God only in a general or vague way, well then, that must mean knowing God isn't very important to us, as life's other concerns supersede. Such is dishonoring and above all things short-sighted and surely in many cases the reason for our character defects and disappointments in life. These unpleasant consequences of our casual attitude toward God, however, are corrective and born of love. To know God, in any event, is to be progressively more like Him, and He suffers from *NO* defects.

I must stop for a minute to address the never-ending stream of hecklers and faultfinders, so to insist, this is not the Gospel according to me; I am fully aware of the dread that should be anticipated by one who puts false words in God's mouth. My thesis is easily verified by the Bible. I have listed only a few reference verses throughout, so to substantiate my points with scripture. I could easily have interrupted the flow of these essays by adding fifty more, but surely, all adult Christians have studied the Bible thoroughly by now and can attest to the trustworthiness of my contentions. So you see that, whether I entice some by encouragement or by trickery, by rivalry or by shame, is not important; what is important is that all men carefully consider God's one and only written revelation to mankind. How many novels will we read? How many movies shall we watch, before we find time for the most important thing in life, knowing God? Shall we continue? But one more thought: if knowing God depends solely on human works such as this, then the reader will never reach his goal, which would in the end prove a loss.

A little about God's character: By definition of His name, the eternal uncreated "I AM'.' God is more than and greater than any list we might compile. But most basically, according to the narrative of holy scripture, I will state two attributes: the seeming paradox of love and justice; these are the bookends that encase all else that God is to us. It is to the degree that we relate to these conditions that we find ourselves balanced or unbalanced in the scales. Let no one think I am saying that we can earn or win by our own efforts this eternal relationship, not at all.

"For by grace you have been saved through faith, and that not of yourselves; it is the gift of God, not of works, lest anyone should boast." (Eph. 2:8–9)

So what of these scales? The scales are God's mysterious scales. He calculates and determines both temporal and eternal realities according to them. First and most crucially our eternal destiny is decided in the scales. Again, not our good deeds versus our bad, for a man who truly receives Jesus Christ as Lord and Savior *will be saved*, even if he confesses such faith on his deathbed, or on His cross, this was the case of one of the men crucified beside Jesus.

Then he (the crucified criminal) said to Jesus, "Lord remember me when you come into your kingdom," and Jesus said to him, "Assuredly, I say to you, today you will be with Me in Paradise" (Luke 23:42–43).

This confessed criminal had no time to counterbalance a lifetime of sin. His reward will be less than the great saints, no doubt, but that is another essay, suffice to say, the lowest station in Heaven is a very good one. Apparently, the judgment of one's salvation is determined by his present sincerity, not his past sins, and that is very good news and it is why we call God "love" and "full of grace." And the balancing satisfaction of "justice" has been paid in full by Jesus's sacrifice, provided we "believe," which is covered in essay 4—"What Equals Belief?"

Secondly, as concerns temporal judgment, if a man who is already saved by faith, but is backslidden and not presently in pursuit of, or cultivating a relationship with God, but rather is living predominantly under his own power and will, then such a man is prone to fail in his character and actions. These will be weighed in the scales and these will be found wanting. These should not be surprised when their temporal/physical lives become hard and unfulfilled, or when their spiritual lives grow flat. Again, this is only a temporary judgment in the case of a saved man—for his own good, so to draw him back home, but this way is hard. I speak from long experience, with profound regrets...But perhaps, questioning my sorted past is shortsighted since it brought me to prison, the place of my most dedicated and uninterrupted study and thus the bulk of my written works to date.

"My son, do not despise the chastening of the Lord, nor detest His correction; for whom the Lord loves He corrects, just as a father the son in whom he delights." (Proverbs 3:11–12)

It is unfortunate, however, that we must be constantly guided like children, even prodded like rebellious, unreasoning beasts of burden. God involves Himself in this long suffering on our behalf because by His nature He is love, but remember that other bookend—justice, for He will not violate it because by His unswerving righteousness, He cannot violate it. Nor should He be thought a harsh Father, what more could He have done for us beyond dying on a cross for our justification in the person of the Son, and just now, He labors in the person of the Holy Spirit to foster an intimacy with us toward our sanctification. Talk about sons and daughters of privilege. We are also kin to the King called Christ, ruler of all the cosmos. However, we are not kin to Him by osmosis in our natural lives, but we are grafted into the family of God by our action of faith, which come by grace. There they are again. Faith and Grace, the two delightful daughters of their Father and ours, but only if we will.

What is grace? Speaking about the unattainable perfection of the strict rules and principles of the Old Testament Law; the Apostle Paul explains a human pattern familiar to all mankind, which, while it should not be misconstrued as promoting compromise or an acceptance of mediocrity, it does comfort us that even the greatest of saints struggled to be holy in their humanity and were humbled enough to admit it. It is Grace through Faith in Christ that covers our past, present, and future sins, presenting us as sons and daughters of God our Father. Listen to the Apostle as he relates his own struggle with holy living and how he ends his lament with reassuring hope of God's grace, which makes full provision for our lack. Notice Paul is speaking in the first person...

"For we know that the law is spiritual, but I am carnal, sold under sin. For what I am doing, I do not understand. For what I will to do, that I do not practice; but what I hate, that I do. If, then, I do what I will not to do, I agree with the law (old testament) that it is good. But now, it is no longer I who do it, but sin that dwells in me. For I know that in me (that is in my flesh) nothing good dwells; for to will is present with me, but how to perform what is good I do not find. For the good that I will to do, I do not do; but the evil I will not do, that I practice. Now if I do what I will not to do, it is no longer I who do it, but sin that dwells in me. I find then a law, that evil is present with me, the one who wills to do good. For I delight in the law of God according to the inward man. But I see another law in my members, warring against the law of my mind, and bringing me into captivity to the law of sin which is in my members. O wretched man that I am! Who will deliver me from this body of death? I thank God—through Jesus Christ our Lord! So then, with the mind I myself serve the law of God, but with the flesh the law of sin." (Romans 7:14–25)

In his letter to the Romans, chapter 3, Paul explains that the Old Testament Law called for perfection in sinlessness, which none of us on our own could ever attain, thus, we can only be saved by God's graceful pardon, which we receive vicariously through faith in His Son, who was sacrificed on our behalf, even though we ourselves have crucified Him. How have we crucified Jesus, you might ask? Simply, it is our individual and collective sins that created the need for Christ's sacrifice. So again to answer the above question, "what is grace?" this is our best example.

"But now the righteousness of God apart from the law is revealed, being witnessed by the law and the Prophets, even the righteousness of God, through Faith in Jesus Christ, to all and on all who believe." (Rom. 3:21–22).

These truths expressed in Roman and elsewhere throughout the Bible are, however, not easily conveyed in words, but are spiritually discerned to those who seek the deep mysteries of God. And make no mistake, simple and common folks (and I am one) can most certainly be so enlightened.

So then, by grace through faith in Christ we find forgiveness from all sin, opening communication with the

Father and the Son through the Holy Spirit. Let's take courage in what time remains, being by our words and deeds heralds of the GOOD NEWS, which is Jesus Christ crucified for the sins of the world; then, on the third day in fulfillment of the Prophets, He rose from the grave, being the first fruits from among the dead, of all who pursue God. In this way, all are graciously called, but only those who will to come are chosen.

"I call heaven and earth as witnesses today against you, that I have set before you life and death, blessing and cursing; therefore choose life, that both you and your descendants may live." (Deut. 30:19).

Finally, to St. Thomas's and our question, "What is God," an absolute answer remains a mystery for the time-being, but as for the how, we might suggest: The most astonishing thing of all is that we exist at all, that anything is here, that here is a place anywhere in time and space, such is an impossibility that just happens to be a true reality, as everyone can attest. God must be somehow like that! But to know Him we must pursue Him, as He is a treasure of infinite value hidden in plain sight, even within us, as surely as we exist breathe and have "consciousness."

Where is God? The Apostle Paul explains that. "He is not far from each one of us; 'For in Him we live and move and have our being'" (Acts 17:27–28). The Bible tells us that God is omnipresent—that is, everywhere. And Jesus unfolds to us the concept that God is within us and so is the Kingdom (Luke 17:21).

So I suppose we may come to know God philosophically in the written Word, or we may behold Him in the flesh in Jesus Christ, or we may sense Him in Spirit every-where, including within ourselves. Truly, it is in seeking that we find, and it is after knocking that the door will be opened. Amen.

Ray Amato
Ocean County Jail, 2013
Toms River, NJ

PURSUING OUR TRIUNE GOD
Essay 2

The mystery called man or humankind is a three-part being: body, soul, spirit. How much might these correspond to the three persons of our triune God: Father, Son, Holy Spirit? I frankly am unsure; perhaps there is little or no correspondence, though I doubt the latter. Anyway, in just a quick and cursory look, some curious and startling similarities strike me. I mean the point that God is three persons in One; while man is one person in whom is contained three elements. Not exactly the same, in fact opposite, nonetheless a striking comparison. Also we will consider three concepts concerning the relationship within the Holy Trinity and their possible correlation with the three elements of man:

1) Our body and Christ the Son
2) Our soul and God the Father
3) Our spirit and the Holy Spirit

First, does Jesus the Son of God who was clothed with a human body suggest significant correlation to the body of man? I would think it must, since God is a Spirit being who at a certain point in time took on a human body in the person of the Son so to simulate with man for various reasons, mostly to become the means of our salvation. But carefully note, Jesus should not be thought to have existed in bodily form before His incarnation in Bethlehem some two thousand years ago, except in the Old Testaments mention of pre-incarnate visitations of "The Angel of God," but that is an altogether different point, and besides these cases occur after creation; in the dispensation of time and space, not in eternity past.

Second, does our omniscient (i.e., all-knowing) God and Father most famously known as master builder of the universe, infinite in knowledge suggest any parallel to the God-given part of man called the brain or soul? I think this has merit, since it is by his very brain or soul that man likewise designs and creates, mimicking God whose image man was created in the likeness of (Gen. 1:26), only of course on an infinitely smaller scale, then too God created everything out of no things, while for his projects creative man has need of the material that God had provided by divine fiat at the time of creation.

Third, does the Holy Spirit resemble the spirit part of man, which is the true essence of the man? While this may seem at first glance to be reasonable due to the use of that same word spirit, I offer that it is also like the other two, a most strained comparison. Bear in mind that while God most times governs the universe by "so-called" natural law (which reasonable man can often understand, even predict), He also intervenes at times acting in the "so-called" super-natural, exhibit #1, the creation of the universe "exhilo"—

that is, out of nothing. This variable called the miraculous may at any time of God's choosing push reason out of the equation. Note: The spirit that God breathed into Adam (Gen. 2:7), which is perpetuated to us in an unbroken chain through birth is not necessarily a spirit unto salvation. It may be an eternal spirit, but not automatically an eternally saved spirit, not that is, unless or until it is filled with or sealed by the Holy Spirit by grace through faith in Jesus Christ our Lord and Savior.

Before going any further, I must say, the mysteries of the Holy Trinity are so profound and ultimately unfathomable that I frankly fear going on in any other way, but with great respect, care, and humility. Not that one's salvation must necessarily hinge on such knowledge, but understanding God more fully should not merely be our privilege but our passion. Certainly, I do not claim to be solving these immemorial mysteries, i.e., God's triuneness, for that would portend such foolish pride as to be laughable; on the other hand, I dislike oversimplifications or skipping over subjects of such great reality and magnitude simply because they are difficult. I dislike even more being spoken to as if I were a child, except of course, if I am humble enough to hear it when I actually behave like a child, which I must admit occurs more often than is becoming of a man, but I digress.

Talks I've heard or works I've read concerning the Trinity always land more toward the philosophic, this probably owing to the point that God has left this mysterious knowledge of himself perhaps above all other mysteries ultimately obscure. This suggests that it's reality is at this time beyond our ability to fully comprehend, which I think is a safe bet. Moreover, since God could have easily made us able to understand all mysteries (all the things, incidentally, that we will understand in glory), it must be that these are ultimately obscured beyond our limits by design. This could be for any number of reasons, not least of which that it affords us opportunity unto faith, also, to afford God the pleasure that can only come to a Father whose children choose to love Him, who run after Him as doting sons and daughters. For the Father could find little pleasure in His children coming to Him after all things were proved, after finding out that their Father owns the cattle on a thousand hills, coming to Him out of selfishness, out of greed, like trite opportunists. For the scriptures assure us of this following thing quite clearly: in addition to being all-loving, all-powerful, all-knowing, and everywhere-present, our Father is a very rich and generous Sire. Only one condition applies—namely, faith in action and Jesus consolidated it so beautifully when He was asked the question, "What must I do to be saved?"

"And you shall love the Lord your God with all your heart, with all your soul, with all your mind, and with all your strength. This is the first commandment. And the second, like it, is this: you shall love your neighbor as yourself. There is no other commandment greater than these." (Mark 12:30–31)

But where we fall short of this perfection we are comforted by the following.

"God to demonstrate at the present time
His righteousness, that He might be just
and the justifier of the one who has faith
in Jesus." (Romans 3:26)

If faith in Christ Jesus is disregarded after revelation, then the God of Heaven and Earth is nothing to that man, except of course a very offended judge whose only begotten Son has been (as far as that man is concerned) slain in vain. This, my friends, is a most egregious and dreadful position to find oneself in upon death and final judgment. But there is hope today as long as it is called today; therefore, it is good for you and me to hear Love's warning. Listen and wonder.

26 "For if we sin willfully *after we have Received the knowledge of the truth*, there no longer remains a sacrifice for sins,

27 but a certain fearful expectation of judgment, and a fiery indignation which will devour the *adversaries*.

28 Anyone who has rejected Moses' law dies without mercy on the testimony of two or three witnesses.

29 Of how much worse punishment, do you suppose, will he be thought worthy who has trampled the Son of God underfoot, counted

the blood of the covenant *by which he was sanctified* a common thing, and insulted the Spirit of grace?

30 For we knew Him who said "Vengeance is mine, I will repay," says the Lord. And again, "The Lord will judge His people."

31 "It is a fearful thing to fall into the hands of the living God." (Hebrews 10:26–31)

Forgive me if I seem to stray from our main topic of the Holy Trinity, so to discuss this other mysterious portion of scripture directly above, which is also difficult. Read all of chapter 10 or the whole book of Hebrews for fuller context.

Question: Might the interpretation be that Jesus's sacrifice has saved *everyone* in theory but then given back with contempt by those who refuse His gospel? It seems the unpardonable sin, if unrepented, is the rejection of Jesus as Christ. For that would solve this looming problem that the book of Hebrews "seems" to contain. That is, the problem of this generic man who has already been saved (for he is called sanctified in verse 29) to "lose" his salvation, which otherwise would seem to fly in the face of the balance of the Bible taken in full context, which according to God's infallibility cannot be the case. For the passage does speak of counting Jesus as a mere man. Remember, the persons committing this sin are called "adversaries," as well as "sanctified" and as Jesus tells us elsewhere, "You cannot serve two masters."

More from the book of Hebrews:

> 36 For you have need of endurance, so that after you have done the will of God, you may receive the promise:
> 37"For yet a little while, and He who is coming will come and will not tarry.
> 38 Now the just shall live by faith; but if anyone draws back. My soul has no pleasure in him."
> 39 But we are not of those who draw back to perdition, but of those who believe to the saving of the soul. (Hebrews 10:36–39)

It would take us to far-off subject to consider all of Hebrews at this time, but it seems to me to be saying that everyone is potentially saved but thrown back defiantly into God's face by those who will not crown Jesus as Lord. By this, they are disqualified to have Him as savior. Put another way, I believe this problem can be reckoned by the fact that while saved people will never attain perfection in this life, they will certainly improve in character as they by faith pursue our triune God which leads to sanctification. But the question is what is the mark (more on this in essay 4). Seems to me, anyway, that some people will not receive salvation because they will not accept it on God's terms, which are the only acceptable terms. We have all heard those proud and belligerent statements or perhaps we ourselves have shaken our puny fists toward Heaven and uttered them ourselves. For example, "Thanks anyway, I don't need God" or that other notoriously famous one,

"I'm a good person, God can take me or leave me," etc., and so on the countless contemptuous blasphemies continue seemingly with no fear of God. In any event, one thing seems sure to me, and that is, that God is too good, too just, too much of a proponent of free will; or shall we say, freedom to force Himself or His eternal Paradise on any such a one, if he/she persist to the end, which of course is to say that the invitation is always open to those who yet live, but that is, an uncertain science, for it is subject to abrupt and violent changes in an uncertain world.

PURSUING OUR TRIUNE GOD
Essay 3

While discussing the three parts of man as having some correlation with the three persons of God, it might seem that the spirit part of man is paramount among the other two parts, i.e., body and soul. For it was the breathing in of the spirit that brought the man to life: "And the Lord God formed the man of the dust of the ground, and breathed into his nostrils the breath of life; and man became a living being" (Genesis 2:7). (The other explanation of man's origin or genesis being offered by evolutionists, atheists, and agnostics is basically as follows: they tell us that the universe that could not have always existed just happened to appear one day all by itself, and that by random chance accident, all the complex systems—from the gigantic star systems, to the microscopic living cell, to the human brain and consciousness—all occurred on their own with no need of a creative designer, even though all these things show phenomenal design. Now if that isn't a fairytale for grownups nothing is, a fairytale for grownups I say, because they use big words and they beguile us with their pedigree and certificates and fancy fraternities). Conversely, the Bible tells us, when the process is reversed and the final breath is breathed out, the physical man dies and the spirit departs. The physical remains remain as an inanimate object returning back to the dust from whence it came. Anyway, to our man of reason I would say, if one allows for that one irreplaceable mysterious phenomena called God, all the rest is quite reasonable.

The Holy Trinity: Father, Son, and Holy Spirit are not only a self-existing unity, but also co-existent, co-equal, and eternal, all are incorruptible and at the risk of being repetitive, indestructible. But for our purpose here, all are spirit; this fact makes our comparison between our Triune God and the three-part being called man diminish precipitously.

Before discussing how God in all three persons are at bottom spirit, some important points should be stated: For all members of the Godhead to be persons in themselves, there must be something to differentiate one from the other. That difference we shall see is in position in the hierarchy and in function.

The Son is equal in essence to the Father for reasons mentioned directly above; however, positionally, He assumes a station or place under the Father's headship. This is clearly spelled out in the whole of the Bible, but most clearly understood in the narrative of the New Testament progressively, as Christ the Son takes on a human body in the form of Jesus of Nazareth. Not only did He serve mankind in His earthly ministry, but also and firstly He served His Father. (Incidentally, it is my understanding that the Father is no one's servant).

Jesus served men and the Father in many ways, to the extreme of dying on a cross for our redemption so that through faith, we too may be sons and daughters of His Father and ours.

The Holy Spirit served the Father by serving Jesus in His earthly ministry and by serving us in our lives and ministries and by revealing the Living Word (Jesus) to us toward our adoption and redemption. Jesus now ministers from the throne room at God's right hand in heaven on our behalf as High Priest. The Holy Spirit now ministers to us here on earth as our counselor, comforter, and teacher, also He is our inward guarantor, revealing that we, in fact, belong, that we are safely saved; but this surety of our unimpeachable salvation comes in reward to the obedient, while the lack of it brings correction, a safeguard drawing us back to divine fellowship and a renewed certainty of our sonship.

For a human example of plurality in unity, we could sight God's claim in Ephesians 5:31: "For this reason a man shall leave his father and mother and be joined to his wife, and the two shall become one flesh." Now if God says that the two become one, then it is settled, but in this unity, even though the man and the woman are spiritual equals in God's eyes, it is also true that the woman finds herself under the headship of the man in the marriage relationship for orders sake, and no, I will not apologize, but I will sight the scriptures, which should settle any misunderstanding: "But I want you to know that the head of every man is Christ, the head of woman is man, and the head of Christ is God" (1 Cor. 11:3). Again, the three persons of God find comparison with the twin unity of the husband-wife relationship; in that the individual members are essential equals, but positionally and functionally different.

But now, what do we mean by saying God is spirit in all three persons?

First, the Holy Spirit is spirit; hopefully there needn't be much difficulty or confusion here. In theological circles, the study of the Holy Spirit is called the study of pneumology; the root word commonly used in medical science has to do with breath or breathing, for instance that lung disease is called pneumonia or in the mechanical vocations air-powered tools are called pneumatic tools. As you recall in Genesis 2:7, the breath of God brought animated life to the man of clay. Also notice how the Holy Spirit is described as coming as wind on the day of Pentecost; the day the Church was born: "And suddenly there came a sound from heaven, as of a rushing mighty wind, and it filled the whole house where they were sitting. Then there appeared to them divided tongues, as of fire, and one sat upon each of them. And they were all filled with the Holy Spirit" (Acts 2:2–4).

Second, the Father is spirit. This also becomes factually plain in the general flow of the whole biblical narrative.

I will sight one example from St. John's gospel, and here John is quoting Jesus as He spoke to the woman at the well in Samaria. "But the hour is coming, and now is, when the true worshippers will worship the Father in spirit and truth; for the Father is seeking such to worship Him. God is Spirit, and those who worship Him must worship in spirit and truth" (John 4:23–24). Now we may picture the Father as an older-looking Jesus, perhaps with a white beard, a handsome and distinguished face, elegantly robed, and seated on an actual pearl white throne, and so on.

While this may be helpful during prayer and meditation, it is inaccurate in reality. Nevertheless, I do not think this an impiety in the least. After all, God judges the intentions of the heart heavily over and above mere legalism. I'll go one more and venture that our Father is delighted with such well intentions from His loving and respectful "little children." How can I be sure, you might ask? Well, besides being a Bible student for many years, I too am a father of four children who were once very young and innocent or, perhaps, better put, naive and at that time far my intellectual inferiors. Again, the analogy is always strained when comparing God and man. In any event, while we may not be able to resist the tendency of picturing God the Father in a human form, it is not the case. Again, I see no harm to it, especially since it can be helpful to our communication, which is so crucial to our spiritual health. Too, for finite human beings living in a material world, comprehending our spirit God without a picture is like trying to comprehend a fourth dimension, or a new primary color, or a cardinal number such as "three," which denoteth not a quantity.

Third, the Son is spirit. This perhaps will require more explanation then the other two since we so often picture the Son in His human form as Jesus; the baby Son of the Virgin Mary, who died on a physical cross, and shed real blood and was resurrected to bodily form. Truly the Son of God became the human Son of Mary, but it was not always this way. Before the world or any created thing existed, our uncreated God existed in all three persons: Father, Son, and Holy Spirit. As we had explained in essay one, the Son as yet had no human form. That great saint and apostle John, through divine revelation brings us back before the creation of the universe in chapter 1:1–2 of his gospel. John here refers to Jesus as he often does as "the WORD"!

"In the beginning was the WORD, and the WORD was with GOD, and the WORD was GOD. He was in the beginning with GOD" (John 1:1–2). On day 6 of creation, we read an inner trinitarian conversation: "Then God said, Let Us make man in Our image…" (Genesis 1:26).

Not very long after the great flood of Noah, we read of an inner trinitarian conversation at the Tower of Babel (now in modern-day Iraq). By now there is a physical world, but it is still long before the incarnation of our Lord Jesus. Yet the Father speaks to the Son, listen.

> "Come, let Us go down and there confuse
> their language, that they may not under-
> stand one another speech." (Genesis 11:7)

And that is why they called the place Babel or Babylon, for the confounding of their language caused them to babble, not understanding one another. To this day, the ancient place is known to us as Babylon. Incidentally, this is a reasonable explanation for the vast diversity of human language, which is otherwise a great mystery.

Later in Old Testament times, we read of a number of pre-incarnate visitations of the Son, though not by a natural birth; it is simply, or not so simply, a miraculous manifestation of the Son of God in the mature state of a full-grown man having no record of birth or genealogy. All this for the advancement of the Father's plan—for a couple of examples:

> "And He (the Son) said, "Your name shall no longer be called Jacob, but Israel, for you have struggled with God and with men, and have prevailed." Then Jacob asked, saying, "tell me your name, I pray," and He said, "Why is it that you ask about my name?" And He blessed him there. So Jacob called the name of the place Penial. "For I have seen God face to face, and my life is preserved." (Genesis 32:28–30)

Another pre-incarnate visitation of the Son of God is in the man Melchizedek, King of Salem and Priest of God Most High. Read about it in Genesis 14:18–20, Psalm 110 esp. vs. 4, Hebrews 5–7.

The facts are clear, however, that before these marvelous manifestations and especially the one in Bethlehem the Son of God was pure spirit. Since then and through eternity future the Son retains His body like His brothers and sisters of the true faith in the true God. Bodies that will forever eat the sweetest fruit, drink the purist water and the finest wine of remembrance, bodies that will touch only the softest garments, smell the most reminiscent fragrances, hear the most heavenly and imaginative music and poetry heretofore unthought of and see views and experience weather so delightful as to be beyond our present comprehension.

What is God?: "Darkness to the intellect
But sunshine to the heart."
(Frederick W. Faber,"The Cloud of Unknowing")
Lord how great is our dilemma! In thy presence
silence best becomes us, but love inflames
our hearts and constrains us to speak.
Were we to hold our peace the stones would cry out;
yet if we speak, what shall we say? Teach us to know
that we can know, for the things of God knoweth no
man, but the Spirit of God. Let faith support us where
reason fails, and we shall think because we believe, not
in order that we may believe. In Jesus's name. Amen.
(A. W. Tozer, "Knowledge of The Holy")

Believing In Christ Equals Salvation
But
What Equals Belief?
An Essay To The Church
Essay 4

Perhaps one of the most unasked questions on the mind of many Christians is, how good or how submissive to God's will must one be to belong to God's family to be saved? I think it's obvious why we don't ask that question out loud; in any event, I will attempt to answer this abstract, spiritually discerned, rarely asked question, no little task. But first three more questions:

1) Do I need to be good at all? Some wrongly think not. They say, "Name it and claim it," or "Once saved, always saved." These are true statements based on the fact that salvation is by grace, but grace is predicated on faith, and faith is an action word showing itself in deeds. See James 2:20–24.

2) Do I need to be perfect? Some, at the other extreme, wrongly think this possible; we might dub them the works righteousness crew or worse

the self-righteous—that is, if they think they have attained it. This is an overzealous reaction due to a partial reading of scripture. They overlook the fact that such a doctrine "eases God out," and its acronym spells "EGO" and that is why pride is at the bottom of all sin.

3) Or does the mark lie between the two extremes? Yes, of course it must. I believe the enemy does his greatest damage by leading us to extremes. He dresses up as an angel of light to deceive; he says to the name it and claim it crew, "Have your cake and eat it too, for God is love," but neglects to say that God is also justice. To the works righteousness crew he says, "You mustn't have any, it is sinful," for he knows full well that many of these things are gifts to be enjoyed with thanksgiving and he knows that through disinformation he can expect to efficiently frustrate many Christians unnecessarily, limiting their communion with our triune God and by extension limiting their good spiritual influence in the world; remember, we have a foe and an ongoing battle to fight and understanding one's enemy is a good start. Such propaganda may come directly from demonic sources or from our well-meaning siblings who themselves have taken the bait.

As for this concept of salvation, and our personal awareness of irrevocably possessing it, though it may surely be known, any explanation for another's salvation remains an abstract concept and ultimately unknowable.

The question is ours alone to answer, for all are invited to the wedding, but it is for God and the man alone to know if they be wed, for when it is genuine, it is knowable. God's perfect judgment of true faith is unique as it varies from person to person due to the continual flux of circumstances surrounding each one's very different life experiences; one is born rich another poor, one well-trained and educated, another as though brought up in a wolf pack, some loved, others abused, etc. In any case, however, the only standard acceptable to a righteous God concerning His children is perfection, which Christ has won for all who believe; His perfect sacrifice covers all that is lacking. Surely we cannot achieve perfection on our own; therefore our just God does not require it, but neither can we live forever in blatant disregard of His law and will, such might be called unfaithfulness or unbelief.

The Pharisees and Sadducees (the civil [secular] and ecclesiastical [religious] leaders of Israel, called the Sanhedrin) being meticulous legalists and hair splinters, asked Jesus a question about authentic faith. They wanted details so they could *"do it"* themselves and of course so to *"enforce it"* on others, but before you can do it, you must be it or be about it, which starts as passively as a decision then swiftly moves into action by a new power, a power born of faith, even the Holy Spirit who is the source of that power; invisible strength, anonymous, subtle and that is why busy people like Pharisees and you and I may totally miss it. So now without further ado, the correct answer, Jesus's answer, which of course must be the final answer:

Then one of them, a lawyer—(Pharisee), asked Him—(Jesus) a question, testing Him, and saying, "Teacher, which is the greatest commandment in the Law?" (Old Testament). Jesus said to him, "You shall love the Lord your God with all your heart, with all your soul, and with all your mind. This is the first great commandment. And the second is like it: You shall love your neighbor as yourself. On these two commandments hang all the Law and the Prophets." (Matt. 22:35–40)

Talk about brilliance in brevity; one would think it should be easy to understand, but apparently not. We should notice that the Lord's answer, to love perfectly God and man is an impossible task, and that is why He died for us as the sacrificial Lamb of God, who of course is God. In full context then, what is implied is that true faith is a growing process; it is not nearly as important where we are along the journey as in which direction we are going. Our salvation is not about our past failures, it's about our present dedication, sincerity, and intentions, always mixed with a contrite and humble spirit.

Life in such a difficult and sinful world is like swimming against the tide of a swift river. If one swims with steadfast conviction, he will make progress, but if he ceases to swim, he will not maintain his progress, but will instead be washed back, losing his testimony in the tumult of its current, needing again to be rescued. I'm glad to say there is a Rock in the midst of this river where a weary swimmer may find refuge—rest for his soul. That Rock is the Lord, the Lion from Zion, the "Rock of Ages" and our liaison to our Father of providence.

The Bible is a reflection of God's character, that perfect mark, but God reveals Himself to man in other ways. These other ways were the available light in prebiblical times and the light to pagans outside of the Bible's influence for many years; in fact to this day, with all our media, some still have never heard the Gospel (Good News). Are they all necessarily lost? Absolutely not! I can already hear those proverbial Belfast bombers cry "HERETIC." I shall give my biblically based explanation shortly.

1) The first and most basic, even tangible evidence of God's existence and His benevolence is attested to by the physical universe, which apart from Him could not exist. So by it everyone may know that "God is."

2) The second revelation is the knowledge of the laws of good and evil, of right and wrong. This is automatically imparted to all mankind in his/her conscience. Even people who never heard of Jehovah or Jesus or the Bible have always had this innate understanding of right and wrong, an essence all about them. People of all eras and cultures throughout recorded history have understood the wrongness of stealing, killing, lying, etc. And they have understood love, kindness, and generosity, etc. Judging by Hollywood, and pseudoscience, one would think ancient man was nothing but a stupid, violent brute, which is not only incorrect but

willful ignorance: very misleading. I would only tell such professors that Confucius, Aristotle, and Abraham lived a long time ago, and they might well have been smarter and kinder than he likes to think of himself, anyway, by conscience we can know to some extent "God's will," either obeying our conscience, or disregarding it. (Read Romans 2:14–15.)

3) The third and most specific revelation is God's written Word, the Bible. One big difference between the pagan with his two forms of revelation and the Christian with his three is more revelation means more responsibility, "For everyone to whom much is given, from him much will be required" (Lk. 12:48). In any case, we do not assume people are better off without the gospel; on the contrary, we are commissioned to carry the gospel to all the world for the three revelations are far and high above the two leading not only to a fuller relationship with God, but also to the preservation and thus continuance of life on Earth, as the Church is called by Jesus, "the salt of the Earth" (Matt. 5:13). And what are salt's properties if not to preserve, to season, and to purify.

> The heavens declare Thy glory, Lord,
> In every star Thy wisdom shines;
> But when our eyes behold Thy Word,
> We read Thy name in fairer lines.
> (Isaac Watts)

Now back to our question, how strict must one adhere to God's will so to be received as genuine, thus saved unto eternal kinship with God? Only one possible answer can be given with total confidence, though you may find it rather vague. The answer we have already stated: it must fall with varying degrees between perfect righteousness since it is unattainable and perfect sinfulness, which is also…unattainable, for even Adolf Hitler was sometimes kind to little German boys and girls and to his dog and his mistress. That I think is as close as we dare come to an absolute answer. Not exactly going out on a limb, I know, but going beyond it is only a presumption of judgment, to which we are denied the right and that has clearly been related to us. Let me say before moving on, we are right to make many judgments in life. Should I befriend this or that person, should I work here, should I marry her—these are necessary judgments; the forbidden judgment then is of another's salvation, or extent of their accountability. Concerning men, ignorance of the written revelation may not save in many cases because men fail in the first two revelations, but with God who knows all, such can and will be considered. "For when Gentiles (Pagans), who do not have the law (the written revelation), by nature do the things in the law, these although not having the law, are a law to themselves, who show the work of the law written in their hearts, their conscience also bearing witness, and between themselves their thoughts accusing or else excusing them" (Romans 2:14–15). The apostle Paul, being the author of the book of Romans, seems to be holding great hope for the pagan Gentiles, those having only the first and second form of revelation. Seems to me, this group which incidentally would contain the majority of people ever born on earth, will be given the opportunity somewhere between death and judgment to accept Christ as Savior in which case the scripture is not broken. Now listen to Paul again in Romans chapter 11: "For I do not desire, brethren, that you should be ignorant of this mystery, lest you should be wise in your own opinion, that blindness in part has happened to Israel until the fullness of the Gentiles has come in. And so all Israel will be saved, as it is written…" (read full chapter). Apparently, true Israelites will also be given the opportunity to accept Christ between death and judgment again so that the scripture is not broken. I believe this strict and, I might add, uncharitable stance of many in the church has confused and demoralized those yet unsaved who just now maybe knocking on her door.

The best alternative by a long shot, however, is salvation specifically founded on Christ through whom we vicariously achieve pardon of all sins, past, present, and future, whether sins of commission (bad things we have done), or sins of omission (things we should have done). By Jesus's sacrificial death on the cross, our ransom was/ is paid in full. He bore our sins in physical and spiritual suffering, and this is necessary to emphasize, for it is the central point of our faith. It suffices to say while we cannot meet the mark of sinlessness in our own effort, we can and are positionally sinless in God's eyes owing to Jesus perfect and all sufficient sacrifice. If this all seems a bit strained or mechanical it is because of the limitations of our intellect, and our language and the vast chasm that exists between this dimension and that of Heaven, as well as some mysteries that have been permitted to continue for whatever good reasons, only God knows.

There still remains this nagging question: if Jesus's sacrifice covers all my shortcomings, then what is the mark on my part? Can I do my will in some cases, disregarding God's will and still be saved? To start with, it is a bad sign if we are preoccupied with this question; nevertheless, the answer must be yes because we all sin unconsciously as well as willfully even after receiving Jesus as Savior, the source and means by which we grow in righteousness; this is the beginning of sanctification, which means to be set apart, apart from the common and joined to God at which point we enter an enhanced two-way communication with Him. To know God is to love God, at which point it is natural to call Him, Father. Everyone knows a good father overlooks a multitude of shortcoming while focusing on the good his child does, remember God wants to save us. He wants Jesus's sacrifice to merit as many souls as will come to Him.

The extent of our good and true intentions marks the extent of our devotion. The quality of our devotion determines our limitations or lack thereof toward relational growth with God and other people created in His image. The Holy Spirit will accomplish many good character gains in us, but only with our free will operating, or better, cooperating. It is in this growing phase that the Holy Spirit burns bright and convincingly within us, transmitting to us the security of our salvation, which we had already received upon our new birth by faith, but the lag depends on us it seems. This knowledge of our salvation means peace, for who can ruin our day when even death yields the greatest gift yet. The Christian life is a triumphant life but rarely realized at a high level by most, including far too often, the writer also, I say with regrets.

So faith in Christ as our Savior is our salvation from an eternal hell, but that harder and rarer faith that crowns Christ as Lord over our life is that which saves us from the hell of this life and from the hell of our personal fears and from self-loathing. While a less committed professor of faith may still be rendered eternally saved, he will not inwardly know it, he will not internally experience it. He may say he believes he is saved because the Bible tells him so, and this may well be true, but the fact remains academic; he does not experience it, he does not really know it, which severely limits the peace, joy, and confidence God longs to bless him with.

My answer to him who asks, "How is it fair that both, the one who tows the line, and the one who does not, that both can be saved? Not only does the carnal or half-committed Christian miss out on the peace which surety of salvation brings, but he must also endure all the stress and consequences of his sins, which most surely will visit upon his physical body, and spiritual spirit being. The less-committed Christian is far from getting over, far from having his cake and eating it too, far from profiting in his compromised living, for he feels the ever-present danger of God's judgment in this earthly life, which will be all very real and uncomfortable; of this condition I can unfortunately testify. To the many backslidden Christians, however, these struggles are a safeguard, a check drawing us back to our "first love," as the Apostle so beautifully put it. Drawing us back perhaps to the day when Grandmother took us to church as a child, when we believed as little children.

In many places, the Bible is encouraging toward imperfect people, but in other places, it declares a lofty perfection, for it is our goal, a few examples:

"Be perfect" says Jesus "as your heavenly
Fathers perfect." (Mt. 5:48)
John tells us; "He who sins is of the devil, for
the devil has sinned from the beginning.
For this purpose the Son of God was manifested, that
He might destroy the work of the devil." (1 John 1:8)
"If we say that we have fellowship with Him, and walk in
darkness, we lie and do not practice
the truth." (1 John 1:6)
"But be doers of the word, and not hearers
only, deceiving yourselves." (James 1:22)

Taken in full context of the whole of scripture, however, one understands these sayings to be our true aim or goal, so to safeguard us from the paralyzing effects of complacency and compromise. Obviously, the perfect mark must be stated: what else might the Bible say? Could it say, perhaps, just sin a little bit and you will be okay? Of course not, such a statement from a holy God would be ridiculous to imagine. Moreover, we all know that saying which exposes our tendency to take advantage, "Give them one inch and they will take a mile." And nearly all of us can relate to taking the mile in full view of God, in spite of His call to holiness and while this is rather disgraceful it does not necessarily disqualify us from salvation. Again the question comes to mind: what equals belief? The answer is faith in Christ, but it is obedience in a growing process, which answers the question inwardly for each individual. God hates sin and compromise, first, because it cost Him His Son. Second, because it disrupts that fellowship between Him and us. Nevertheless He is patient, even loving toward sinners:

> "God is long suffering toward us,
> not willing that any should
> perish but that all should come to
> repentance." (2 Peter 3:98)

We should thank Him also for our angels who protect us from ravenous demons, which our recklessness would otherwise expose us to, again. I know this too according to the Word and long personal experience.

Is it now becoming clear, just how wrong our attitude would be if our aim was to find the limit we could sin and yet be saved? To sneak in just under the wire, so to speak.

> Jesus said, "No one can serve two masters." (Mt. 6:24)
> "And if a house is divided against itself, that
> house cannot stand." (Mk. 3:25)

This idea of playing two sides is the outlook and method of a user or a con man, not the way of a devoted son or daughter, besides God cannot be conned.

Salvation is offered freely and evenly to all men, as the scriptures so plainly state:

"God shows personal favoritism to
no man." (Galatians 2:6)
"God shows no partiality." (Acts 10:34)

"I call heaven and earth as witnesses today against you, that I have set before you life and death, blessing and cursing: therefore choose life, that both you and your descendants may live; that you may love the Lord your God, that you may obey His voice, and that you may cling to Him, for He is your life and the length of your days..." (Deut.30:19–20a)

"For since, in the wisdom of God, the world
through wisdom did not know God, it pleased
God through the foolishness of the message preached
to save those who *believe*." (1 Cor. 1:21)

It seems reasonable then, with such ample opportunity and an ongoing invitation, that after a lifetime of refusing God, God will grant one's wishes, not forcing Himself on that man against his free will, for eternity.

If someone says, "I love God," and hates his brother, he is a liar, for he who does not love his brother whom he has seen, how can he love God whom he has not seen? And this commandment we have from Him: that he who loves God must love his brother also. (1 John 4:20–21)

Love for each other is love for God and the benefit is built in, whether that love is reciprocated from men or not. If I love another, I experience that love. If I hate another, I experience that hate. The one I love or the one I hate, may or may not feel or respond to my love or my hate, but I am sure to be affected by it. Love is liberating and forgiveness is freeing, and both are a sign that our belief is genuine; it is the true mark of a Christian. If we have such a desire, we are born of God and sustained by Him, even grown by Him in the direction of perfection, and we will know our salvation is secure, that we have chosen to live, and that we will live eternally, as sure as we are twice born through faith in Jesus Christ our Savior.

King Solomon tells us, "Faithful are the blows of a friend, but deceitful are the kisses of an enemy" (Prov. 27:6).

Consider this then, the blows of a friend, but the kisses of liberal theology, pseudoscience, and secular humanism as the kisses of death, or at least the kiss of confusion.

Incidentally

There is no perfect church. Not the Catholic Church, or the Protestant, not the Orthodox, or the conservative, or the Pentecostal, nor any other. I have been to many of them and thoroughly agree with Dr. Billy Graham, who said, "There is no such thing as a perfect church, but if you or I were ever to find one and joined it, it would then become imperfect." So let's dismount the high white charger. These judgments so commonly spoken against other individuals and other denominations are nothing short of sickening, as well as, the reason for our universal weakness, at well more than 2 billion professors strong in aggregate. Judging each other, then, is a grave mistake; what do you suppose will come of one who condemns the collective masses strictly out of hand based merely on legalism?

Remember our Lord Jesus's own words:

> "For with what judgment you judge,
> you will be judged: and with
> the measure you use, it will the
> measured to you." (Mt. 72)

So the Apostle Paul asks; "Why destroy yourself?"

You know it seems that those of us who had so clearly miss the mark of perfection are protected from this particular hypocrisy, but the self-righteous and assumed self-proclaimed orthodox are often in greater danger at this point it seems.

Ray Amato
From behind the wall at
Bayside State Prison, Leesburg, NJ
Presented at chapel service
November 2009

Ray Amato
Aug. 2013, OCJ
Toms River, NJ

"Spiritual Reality"

"For we walk by faith, not by sight."
—2 Corinthians 5:7

To be spiritually directed may bring to mind many ideas. Stating what may sound like an opinion to those earthbound naturalists may be to the spiritually borne a known truth or principle. Two examples will be offered, first a short proverb directly below, then an essay. Both will be indications of what I propose to be "Spiritual Realities."

Refined and Real
Like a rough diamond
lately mined.
Or a dray horse
Newly born,
So it goes with people;

That which is not put through a process
cannot be "REFINED."
And that which is not tested
is not "proved" genuine.
(Incidentally, the proof is for our personal
information, not God's, who is omniscient.)

"Spiritual Reality"
An Essay

We Follow the Spirit of Revelation, Not Necessarily Our Emotions, Nor Is It Intellect Alone

The unerring scriptures say: "For where two or three are gathered in My (Jesus) name, I am there in the midst of them" (Matt. 18:20). Now we may deduce that the place where Christians gather in Christ's name so to commune with the Father by the indwelling presence of the Holy Spirit—is the "Church." Not of course a building, but a kind of living organism, the body as it were of Christ, of which He is the head. This is sound "theology." Father, Son, Holy Spirit, three persons or personalities of our tri-une God; tri-(three)une-(one). An impossible concept for any mere mortal man, or once-born man to understand, or really come to think of it, for any man to understand for that matter, but not impossible to believe for the twice born man. The Apostle Paul explains, "But the natural man does not receive the things of the Spirit of God, for they are foolishness to him; nor can he know them, because they are "spiritually discerned" (1 Cor. 2:14).

Communion between regenerated souls and the eternal Holy Spirit should be expected to produce extra-natural results. Among them are (and especially with new converts) hope, charity, compassion, a sense of security, and a new sense of meaning in life. As a result of these gifts comes a new and intangible peace, but experience finds an invariable contrary constant tirelessly at work. It is the "yin and the yang" of the far eastern Buddhist, it is called "Karma" by the Hindu sage of the Indian subcontinent, but more specifically it is the ever present conflict of "good and evil" in the teaching of the Galilean Shepherd (and it is not manichaerism or duelism.) This true concept of good vs. evil, however, has always had their naysayers, not least of which are the Atheistic-Nihilists who don't even know that they don't know. "In a meaning-less world where all is automatic and *natural*," they say, "good and evil cannot exist," and the agnostic true to his name says, "If good and evil are real they cannot be known," at least the agnostic knows that he doesn't know, he is therefore less the enemy of truth, I suppose.

It is, however, no mystery to God, nor should it be to us, that good and evil most certainly are real concepts, propagated by real entities. The missionary apostle St. Paul explains in some detail the nature, assumed authority and motives of spiritual beings (evil ones in this instance):

> "For we do not wrestle against flesh and blood, but against principalities, against powers, against the rulers of the darkness of this age, against spiritual hosts of wickedness in the heavenly places." (Eph. 6:12)

Friends, if these foes which we wrestle with in the maintenance of our character are not "flesh and blood," then they are demon spirits, we might even call them "aliens" on the planet, but that is another essay altogether. And even when evil presents itself in flesh and blood men it is under the influence of demons that we act (yes, I said *we*), whether directly, or as evil is ingrained in our culture. The above verse goes on speaking of "principalities," this word denotes assigned territories to officials of various rank who rule there with all the terror and craft of a field marshal. Therefore we could rightly call Satan the commander in chief over a vast army comprised of demonic officers of rank who are over a multitude of infantry soldiers. The Apostle goes on in his outing of this covert enemy calling them "powers" and "rulers of darkness," too, they are "spiritual hosts," hosts of course meaning a great number and they inhabit "the heavenly places," the heavenly places as concerns us here are in the first heaven. Elsewhere in 2 Corinthians 12, Paul speaks of the third heaven which is clear in the text to be God's heavenly realm, AKA "The Kingdom." The second heaven then would be outer space, the cosmos. The first heaven finally, that dwelling place of demons and angels, that spiritual battlefield is the ether, that is, in the very atmosphere of planet earth, the very air we breath. In yet another passage Paul calls Satan, "The prince of the power of the air, the spirit who now works in the sons of disobedience" (Eph. 2:28).

On many occasions, according to scripture, Jesus Himself calls Satan the "ruler" and "prince of this world." Example, John 16:11.

In retrospect then, we find the beginning of understanding made more clear in our personal experience, especially enhanced now as we have established scriptural precedent of both good and evil basic though the course may be.

Jesus is the Good Shepherd, but He is also a King, the commander-in-chief over a host of angels of various rank heroic and might, also in this army are saved men and women. Does this sound mythical or even like a fairytale? First off, myths and fairytales have been great tools of teaching since time immemorial, but what we are dealing with is not only good for learning, but literally true. Granted, these revelations are limited, so is our intellect and the scope of our language, leaving certain mental pictures open to individual imaginations, but the general truths implied are just that, truth, spiritual realities that are spiritually discerned, which brings us back to the thesis of this essay.

While fighting under Heaven's banner and God's command on this physical/spiritual battlefield, we should not expect that the enemy will take any of this lying down. That other great apostle and leader of the early Church, St. Peter gives us good council and fair warning:

> "Be sober, be vigilant; because your "adversary" the devil walks about
> Like a roaring lion, seeking whom he may devour." (1 Pet. 5:8)

To show just how seriously sinister this war is and just how evil natural men can be acting under the influence of demons; we could mention Nero, Attila, Napoleon,

Hitler, Mao, Stalin, etc., or we could consult the traditions (i.e., writing of the early Church Father), which tells us of Peter's eventual crucifixion and of Paul's beheading, it tells us of Justin's martyrdom and of thousands more, also the book of "Acts" tells of many disciples wrongful imprisonment, and that James was put through with a sword, and of the stoning to death of St. Stephen. This is not just an old thing, however; it was a plague and a painful part of faith in the early Church true enough, but it has never subsided. For people are still being imprisoned and killed for their faith all over the world, but most profoundly in the Muslim Middle East and Africa and in Atheist-run states in the Far East, or in the predominantly Hindu territories.

In the paradoxical mix of blessing and persecution these faithful were more than conquerors, and so will we be as we follow our paradoxical leader. Paradoxical, in what way? Jesus is the "Lamb" of God, slain for the forgiveness of our sins, but He is also the "Lion" from the tribe of Judah and the ultimate conqueror. Jesus's "Kingship" is accentuated in Matthew's gospel, but His "Servanthood" is held paramount in St. Mark. He is the "Deity" in John's gospel, but the "Man" in the gospel of Dr. Luke. No doubt the lion will lie down with the lamb, but not just yet. In the meantime, the art of Christian living is to be lamblike, to turn the other cheek, as well as to fight like a fearless lion both in their proper turn; this is not contradictory and Jesus is our only perfect example of it, as He was meek in His own defense to the extreme of crucifixion, but He was fierce in defense of His Father's honor and in defense of the fatherless. We most certainly will win after our earthly struggle, as sure as God the Creator is above Satan the created; nevertheless, we must expect to suffer temporal loss. Even our Lord was wounded in the flesh, being hung on that cruel tree on Calvary's hill, but here now comes the ultimate paradox: He triumphs by that same cross, three days later in the Resurrection, sealing the fate of those who fight against God unto eternal chains of banishment, and sealing the faithful unto eternal life. Heaven is where God is and hell is where He is not and for the lost I say with sadness there will be no comfort, for the un-blessedness will be lonely and sad. At the judgment, the lost will finally have their proof that God and His Heaven are real that will bring only dread and a curse upon the date of their conception, that day when their eternal spirits were granted.

Maybe God doesn't need to record everything about men's lives, maybe it is all recorded in our memory, perhaps He looks into our pupils, that is, into our brain and reads the tape, but really He wouldn't need to, for with 100 percent of our brains capacity open to us, we will recall everything we ever saw, heard, spoke, or did, so that we will understand fully and judge ourselves, leaving the Throne Room either filled with inexpressible joy, or with our stomachs sour, as we finally judge ourselves correctly and simply walk away with profound regret. I don't know.

Speaking to that serpent (the devil) in the Garden at Eden God prophesied concerning his future clash with Jesus at Calvary: "He" (Christ) "shall bruise your head" (a fatal blow) "and you shall bruise His heel (a relatively minor and temporary flesh wound) (Gen. 3:15).

While it is true that Satan, a mere created being, bruised our eternal Lord Jesus in a literal sense, we should keep in mind that God permitted this for redemptive purposes, not because there is any real comparison. My point is, we too should expect to suffer in this life at the hands of such crafty and powerful beings as demons. This alone should drive us to our knees and into the protective arms of our Father, but these things get lost in a busy life, I myself need to pay more attention, to pray more.

We said early on that experience shows that fellowship with God produces joy, hope, surety, and a new meaning to life (especially among new converts). But that without fail that sure hope and joy is often stolen, perhaps later in a lonely place or in our sleep. It is common in the morning upon first sun that one finds the demons have ravaged him with fiery darts of doubt, pessimism, confusion, disappointment, and to some unfortunates dark depression. These have come to usurp or supplant God's rightful place in the man or woman's life. Being inexperienced solders they may not know that it was the flim-flam man sowing seeds of doubt where seeds of faith had so recently sprouted tender and green. Not knowing these things about his enemies' tactics the new Christian (or any Christian) may doubt the genuineness of his communion with God quite unnecessarily.

Notice the method Satan used against our first mother, the naive and innocent Eve: "Hath God really said?" Gen. 3:1). Here he questions God. Then the serpent said to the woman. "You will not surely die" (Gen. 3:4); here he lies by calling God a liar. "For God knows that the day you eat of it your eyes will be opened, and you will be like God, knowing good from evil" (Gen. 3:5); here he tempts Eve by pride. "She took of the fruit and ate" (Gen. 3:6). He deceived Eve, then Adam, and now us? I do not even think Adam and Eve knew that the serpent was their foe, but by now we should!

We can counter these various attacks in two ways: first, by exercises in faith—i.e., divine communion, more specifically prayer: mediation, fellowship, and study, bringing growth. Second is to irrevocably clam the ground and knowledge we have with the Spirit's help already gained. What I mean is simply this: if in the company of the Church and the Holy Spirit we are convinced of some truth, then it is spiritually discerned truth, as it also aligns itself soundly with the infallible scriptures. What greater guarantee of truth could there be? Especially when weighed against the unsound properties of the doubting source, namely, that ever-present, ever-fickle human attribute—emotion. The truth is the truth, but emotions are as unsure a pedestal as the deep blue sea, and only our Lord could stand on that. High emotions are a nice hiatus when they come, but not to be counted trustworthy as a barometer to measure or judge truth. Even within the church walls experience and emotion can lie or be mistaken. I just so happen to have a true story on that one.

One day, I happened to visit a church populated by our more charismatic brothers and sisters of the Pentecostal persuasion. Apparently on the bill that day was, "Joy in the Spirit," and boy I'm telling you it seemed to be working: some of the folks were being, as they call it, "slain in the

Spirit." They were rolling on the floor laughing uncontrollably. The rest were clapping and singing, or else speaking in tongues. In all sincerity, I do not want to sound skeptical, for who am I to judge? In fact, joy in the Spirit as it works itself out in worship is a beautiful thing and no doubt a clear biblical prescription in its proper time as it expresses itself in the entire body and in each individual. However, one man being slain in the Spirit began to weep instead of laugh. Now again, who am I to judge, but this man seemed every bit as sincere as the others if not perhaps more so since he could not be accused of following the crowd, and besides sorrow just seems so much more sincere than hilarity, but not always. Anyway, to my surprise those elders overseeing the whole affair seemed to coldly dismiss this man as one perhaps not aligned with the Holy Spirit. I guess that particular day those "leaders" (I use the word loosely) decided the Holy Spirit ought to minister according to their strict directions, perhaps that the God of the universe should on that day be detained and contained in a certain little box labeled joy. In any event, many sincere people see things many different ways, but emotions are not the judge of God's presence or movements in the church, and in the interest of balance, no one should judge anothers emotions either, but the former is a far more egregious offense.

We all know from experience that emotions can lie; therefore, they need to be told where to get off whenever they would to mislead us. Demons use emotions successfully against us when we become tricked into questioning and doubting formerly discovered truths, via intrusive feelings or emotions which are; at the risk of being repetitive, so unsure.

We should take courage in this: Evil forces have plagued even the greatest of saints down through the ages, and as I understand, many times unproportionately so, with doubts, physical maladies, downer feelings, and even severe mental depression, which I am convinced, at least sometimes can be attributed to demonic attacks. Those known to us today as great saints are so largely because they held tight to the truth in the face of temptations and trials, such as those lies of emotions and feelings which are so nebulous and uncertain, incidentally, these saints, and apostles, and church fathers are not to be prayed to in my judgment, since there is but one mediator between God and man: our Lord Jesus Christ (1 Timothy 2:5), and since no other scriptures point us in that direction. They are, however, held up by the Church for good reason; mostly to learn from, not only as in the case of the apostles, from their biblical writings, or in the case of the rest from their poetry, hymns, essays, and volumes of theology but also to learn from their examples of conduct especially under the hot fire of persecution. When fed to hungry lions or crucified or burned alive at the stake, they did not yield to their very real emotions of fear by changing their allegiance, which could have saved their physical lives, not at all. Rather they held tight unto "faith," which is defined, believing in things unseen, and this is granted by grace to believe by faith, the product of which is eternal security and the inner knowledge of it. Many people don't know what we have already pointed out that suffering, false imprisonment, and martyrdom still occur frequently and massively in so many foreign lands. I pray we never experience such extremes in our God-blessed United States, but that we have and will continue to be tested is as certain as this spiritual war in which we are just now embroiled. Just as fire that tests and purifies all kinds of metals and dray horses, so too, the fire of suffering proves and improves the metal of our faith. In fact, whenever and wherever the Church is most severely tested by said fires, it is then and there that the Church is at its purest, and strongest and where it experiences the most rapid growth in numbers and potency (another spiritually discerned reality, another paradox of Christianity).

Returning to where we began, I believe these above utterances to be trustworthy. Again, the first and most full-proof test of truth when considering any spiritual statement is, does it square with scripture? The second test counts on the writers or readers clear understanding of those very scriptures and his oneness with the Holy Spirit.

But I'm afraid that to understand either, one must establish a relationship with God, not one empowered primarily by human association but rather quickened by the Holy Spirit, through faith in Jesus Christ, all to the glory of our God and Father, amen. It is in this way that one comes to know God, and it is in this way that he can know that he knows; this is the greatest gift in life, outdone only by the gifts to come.

One final thought, concerning that "Charismatic Revival" I had attended, I ask a question. Is our Sprit God only happy all the time? Truth is, after the second coming, that is, after the final judgment or the separating of the lambs and the goats, God will be perpetually joyous all the time most definitely, but until then, during this present dispensation of free will in a warlike atmosphere among good and evil, God's experience is joy and sorrow in the mix of said good and evil. We should keep in mind, while charity, love, and forgiveness pleases Him, as well as our obedience in brotherly love and in our praise and worship toward Him, He also experiences every evil that visits upon His creation, even upon every man. He experiences the weight upon all mothers' soul who must endure the sight of their dying children, those thousands dying of starvation on a garden planet, those thousands dying every day from diseases that are easily avoided or cured, those thousands who are killed or maimed in wars that have never ceased since time immemorial, or thousands lost in drug addiction and the occult, etc., add to these, all animal suffering and universal decadence and it might be true; the tears of that one man at that charismatic revival meeting, I mean. For if the Holy Spirit's emotions are truly being expressed, then it would seem quite right that both laughter and tears would be made manifest among those possessed of God's Spirit, as life occurs in this magnificent yet calamitous world in which we live, where birth and love continue alongside death and hate; this is truly a spiritual war in which we are involved. The war is both physical and spiritual; this is a spiritual-discerned reality and is, I believe, for this reason a most trustworthy truth.

Ray Amato
Feb. 2016
South Amboy, NJ

ON FORGIVENESS AND
BEING FORGIVEN

I know that I am about to make a boastful fool of myself as I tell of my high capacity in forgiving others when they trespass against me. But now I will redeem myself as the Apostle also did by saying that "my boast is in the Lord." God gives gifts to all people, many and various gifts, for as the Apostle informs us elsewhere: "One has this gift and another that." My favorite gift is the forgiveness one because it is in forgiving others that we will in the end find that we have been forgiven and seeing that I was not so highly gifted in some other areas of my life and conduct such forgiveness from a Holy God would seem indispensable.

I have more than a few stories where my God-given capacity to forgive others even confounded me; here I will retell one:

When I was about seventeen, a few friends and I were hangin' on the tracks—as they say, just a smoken an' a jokin' and drinkin' a little too much too. See what I mean about the weaker gifts. Anyway, me and one of my company engaged in what you might call a philosophic difference of opinion, I honestly don't recall what it was, but all on a flash my "friend" Jerry who was seriously training as a kick boxer blind side blasted me with a roundhouse to my left eye, splitting my eyelid in half, instantly putting me to sleep. Like a tilted pinball machine, I tumbled and rolled down a hill from the tracks, waking up in the curb of a busy road to a dizzy blur of headlights in my bloodied eyes. That reminds me of another generous gift to me, I mean, just the finest bunch of guardian angels; I really did run them ragged across the years. Anyway, the following day, I, with four stitches in my left eyelid and a pirate patch, went lookin' for Jerr. And I don't mean so to forgive him, but don't you know that strange yet familiar essence came over me; as we neared and as he noticed the damage, he appeared to me to be truly of a contrite heart. "Sorry," he said in so many words, "but you appeared scary like to me so I threw first." I was strangely no longer angry as I shook his extended hand. I'll keep it real by saying we were never close thereafter, but I definitely, by God's grace, forgave him. And it's a good thing too, since by my own indiscretions in life I have given God the proverbial black eye far too many times to count, regrettably.

Incidentally, I say with a heavy heart, Jerry was murdered about fifteen years later in the violent streets of Newark, NJ. He was blindsided, a knife in the back. I recall Jesus's words of warning which now ring clear and true:

> "Put your sword in its place, for all who take the sword will perish by the sword." (Matt. 26:52)

I think the following is true among people of faith, that he who is forgiven much, loves much—to the extreme toward others who sin against him. I think that people who don't easily forgive others are ignorant of the fact that they also are heavy offenders, for even a slight off-white looks rather tarnished when compared to pure-white, again to the Apostle for conformation:

> "For we dare not class ourselves or compare ourselves with those who commend themselves. But they, measuring themselves among themselves, are not wise." (2 Cor. 10:12)

What Paul is saying is measure yourself to God and see your true neediness, for at bottom every sin is ultimately an offense against Him—Him, who forewarns us that He will judge us with the same severity as we judge others. That is why Jesus blistered those self-righteous religious hypocrites with these following words of warning, saying, "The thieves, drunkards and prostitutes will enter the Kingdom of Heaven ahead of you." Not long after Jesus spoke these words to them, they crucified Him. Most astoundingly, these men too may be saved by the holy blood that they spilled, if they be truly repentant with faith. Simply stated, "Mercy triumphs over judgment," says Jesus, and that is a good place for imperfect people to place themselves.

Now to further sharpen my point, I present our best and only perfect example of forgiveness; of course I'm speaking of Jesus, the sinless, sacrificial Lamb of God, who

Himself is God. And I am thinking especially of that time when He hanged on that cruel tree, where He said on behalf of His crucifiers, "Father forgive them, for they know not what they do" (Luke 23:34). But this forgiveness we are told is predicated on Faith which is by grace received, what a glorious mystery!

Please do not think as many are in the habit of thinking, that, meekness is weakness. Our Lord was meek as He also calls us to be.

Example:

Jesus says "Take My yoke upon you and
learn from Me, for I am gentle
and lowly in heart, and you will find rest
for your souls." (Matthew 11:29)

In this next one, Matthew is quoting Isaiah 62:11 who five centuries earlier prophesied our Lord's Triumphal entry into Jerusalem; the day we now celebrate as Palm Sunday.

Tell the daughter of Zion,
'Behold, your King is coming
to you,
Lowly, and sitting on a
donkey,
a colt, the foal of an ass.
(Matthew 21:5)

Then again, Jesus from His 'Sermon on the Mount" where He said,

> "Blessed are the meek, for they shall inherit
> the Earth." (Matthew 5:5)

Please note, in the above meekness is presented as a virtue, it is more like power under control, and it is not always passive. Again to the WORD we go for conformation. Jesus was more like a lion than a lamb on more than one occasion; true, He was lamb like in His own defense and the cross is our best example, since He could have summoned a legion of mighty angels to His defense but that would have left us in the lurch. Instead, as passively as a lamb, He suffered the most degrading and painful form of execution. On the other hand, Jesus was like a lion in defense of His Father's honor, and in defense of the fatherless, as when He chided His own disciple who shunned the little children from coming to Him (Matt. 19:14). And again in defense of His Father's honor to the tune of overturning tables in the outer court of the Temple, then He said,

> "It is written, 'My house is a house of
> prayer', but you have made it a den of
> thieves.'" From Luke 19:46, quoting
> Isaiah 56:7, Jeremiah 7:11)

You know, they don't call Jesus "The Lion of the tribe of Judah" for nothing. But it is so far only in Him that the lion and the lamb have meet in perfect harmony, yet starkly contrasted, as Mr. Chesterton so aptly put it, "like the red and the white upon the shield of Saint George," who incidentally was not only considered by the church to be an outstanding saint but also a warrior king, both in their proper turn. True, someday the lions will lie harmoniously among the lambs, but not just yet. This I think becomes immediately apparent to all honest observers.

Only perfect people can afford to be severe judges and no man save one was ever perfect nevertheless, He remains a most gracious forgiver toward the faithful who are by His sacrificial blood cleansed to the preservation of their eternal souls, amen. Captain Newton's famous hymn says it well:

> "Amazing Grace, how sweet the sound
> that saved a wretch like me."

Now the facts are that John Newton was formerly a drunkin' rascal and a scalawag and a skipper of a slave trade sailing vessel, but the irony is that if he really meant what he wrote, then he will enter the Kingdom along with those other repentant prostitutes, thieves, and drunkards ahead of those "pretty good" self-righteous ones. For no matter how good one is, he can never earn his place in heaven. For even to think such treads heavily the precious blood of our Lord, for nothing could offend the Father of a sacrificially slain son more thoroughly. It is perhaps the most hideous and foolish sin because one cannot buy ones salvation and one cannot earn it either.

Salvation is a fully-paid-for, free gift; it is freely received with thanks and adoration toward God or it is not receivable. It is of utmost importance to understand that it will not go well for those who pridefully throw so great a gift back into God's gracious face. You've all heard the pomposity before: "No, thanks, I'm good enough. God can take me or leave me." That is a most uninformed statement for at that point no worthy sacrifice remains—dread dread indeed. We should try always to come closer to God's perfect mark, granted, and this for God's good pleasure, but if one thinks he fails not greatly at this point, it is a looming problem, because you know that those who are pretty pious and upstanding people should plainly admit that this is one of their strong gifts, for which they also did not earn or pay a price. And what has King Solomon the wise assured us of:

"For there is not a just man on
earth who does good
And does not sin." (Ecclesiastes 7:20)
And what does Paul say in the New Testament:
There is none righteous no,
not one. (Romans 3:10)

Now what is implied in the balance of Holy Scripture is an assurance that no guilty sinner can endure God's holy presence nor will he suffer us in such a condition. But if we be, by faith, washed in the blood of the Lamb, then we are purified by His merit on the cross, and by none of our own merit. The amount of foolish self-pride needed to mess this one up could sink a battleship. God help us, for it is a dreadful thing to fall into the hands of a jilted and angry God.

King David advises us well, saying,

> "Kiss the Son, lest He (the Father) be
> Angry.
> And you perish in the way,
> When His wrath is kindled
> but a little.
> Blessed are all those who put
> their trust in Him." (Psalm 2:12)

In recap, there are two plain and simple concepts to grasp as concerns this most crucial/central point of Christian faith.

1) We can only be forgiven by grace through faith in Jesus Christ our Lord and Savior.
2) We must forgive others as we also wish to be forgiven.

Ray Amato
10/8/13
Toms River, NJ

UNCHAINED

Be Wise as Serpents and Harmless as Doves
(Matt. 1:16b)

Put not off until tomorrow what should be done today. For any day to which you can ever do anything at all will always be called today. Otherwise, two or more decades may pass in a dizzying maze of disappointment, sorrow, and under-achievement until one finally wakes from his slumber to find he is nearly an old man and that his children have grown without him. Then, my friend, you will mourn with bitter tears, but such rain has been known to bring germination unto new life. If you are in the midst of this desert wilderness, remember, no matter how harsh its pruning treatment may be, it is your place of preparation unto salvation's sanctification, if you will, but only if you will.

For example:

Moses spent forty years in exile tending sheep, in the desert wilderness before meeting God on Mount Sinai in the burning bush, where he received his commission as Israel's deliverer (Exodus chapter 3).

The nation Israel was forty years on the deserted Sinai Peninsula being prepared to enter the Promised Land (Numbers 14:33).

Moses was forty days and nights on Mount Sinai receiving The Commandments (Deuteronomy 9:9).

Long before Moses, in the days of the deluge, in the day of Noah, it rained forty days and nights (Genesis 7:4).

After John baptized Jesus in the river Jordan, Jesus was led immediately by the Holy Spirit into the desert to be tempted forty days and nights by the devil (Matthew 4:1–11). And I bet He prayed a lot during those forty days, like a Christian prisoner in solitary confinement, not such a bad time, can anyone say amen?

After Jesus's execution, the disciples spent forty frightening days in preparation for their dangerous ministry of Church building (Acts 1:3–5).

And so it is by similar paths that all saved people come to the "Marriage Supper of the Lamb." By God's chastening discipline, we are pruned and proved by His grace; our eyes are opened with a salve of the Physician's own making. He is doing for us what we ourselves could not, namely love ourselves, the first step toward loving God and others, which of course is the evidence of a truly enlightened/saved person. Only now, we need to forgive everyone, as we in Christ, have been forgiven, taking courage in the todays which remain, for as far as time is concerned, a lot remains. In fact, for those who follow hard after God the future is infinite and the word infinite is not only indicative of quantity of time, but also of its quality. So high is the quality of our future eternal home that the great Apostle Saint

Paul strains to explain that glimpse of Heaven which God through a vision, had shown him:

> "Eye hath not seen, nor ear heard, nor have entered into the heart of man, the things which God has prepared for those who love Him." (Corinthians 2:9)

Apparently, the aesthetic beauty of God's Heaven is beyond the expression of human language and comprehension. The music and the food, the scents and the sights, the new colors and the light of the place by which we will see—magnificent light, otherworldly light, for God himself is the source of the light in the New Jerusalem.

> "For behold, I create new heavens and a new earth;
> And the former shall not be
> remembered or come to mind.
> But be glad and rejoice forever in what I create;
> For behold, I create Jerusalem as a rejoicing,
> And her people a joy.
> I will rejoice in Jerusalem,
> And joy in my people;
> The voice of weeping shall no longer be heard in her,
> Nor the voice of crying." (Isaiah 65:17–19)

And as sure as God's Word; all true Christians are grafted into Israel through faith in Christ, as the Apostle Paul explains in Romans chapter 11.

Now in view of God's promises given through the Old and New Testament prophets, can you conceive just a little, the healing balm, which is to come upon all the people of all the nations in all the generations in the eternal New City? Consider if you will, the joy in the hearts of those who have lived their lives completely blind or deaf or crippled. Consider the parents who lost children and infants to disease or accident or violence, picture them—picture us entering through the beautiful Pearl Gates of the Celestial city embracing in rapturous joy! Picture the healing blessedness of those formally mentally ill (a far larger group then is now perceived), those abused, mentally retarded, the chronically depressed, the un-beautiful, the harshly judged, and other outcasts, etc., and we all qualify to some extent; for this life spares no one from profound heartache. Listen to Mr. Cohen's clairvoyant glimpse:

Jesus was a sailor
When He walked upon the water
And He spent a long time watching
From His lonely wooden tower
It was then He knew for certain
Only drowning men could see Him
So He said all men shall be sailors then
Until the sea shall free them.
(Leonard Cohen)

God loves all mankind, but to read His word you might think He loves the sick and the lame, the poor and the sinner best, but this is not so, listen:

> Then Peter opened his mouth and said: In truth, I perceive that God shows no partiality.
> But in every nation whoever fears Him and works righteousness is excepted by Him." (Acts 10:34–35)

And Paul tells us: "God shows personal favoritism to no man" (Galatians 2:6).

It works out this way, because the needy are more inclined to humility, but the rich are often self-deceived, under the delusion of self-sufficiency. Listen to our Lord:

> Now it happened, as Jesus sat at the table in the house that behold, many tax collectors and sinners came and sat down with Him and His disciples. And when the Pharisees saw it, they said to His disciples "why does your Teacher eat with tax collectors and sinners?" When Jesus heard that, He said to them, "those who are well have no need of a physician, but those who are sick. But go and learn what this means: I desire mercy and not sacrifice'. For I did not come too call the righteous, but sinners to repentance. (Matt. 9:10–13)

Additionally the Apostle Paul informs us: "None are righteous, no not one" (Rom. 3:10), which can also be translated, none are righteous, not even you or me. Then he implies elsewhere, that to those who think that on their own they have achieved righteousness. The "WAY" is closed.

The above is but one among many examples of Jesus gracing the presence of sinners. The other group He called on frequently were the sick and lame. Question, has a healthy body, mind, and spirit become a curse? Of course not, but these healthy, wealthy and wise are vulnerable to that deadly elective curse called pride, which is the antithesis of humility and humility is the gracious mother of Faith; onto the heirs of life.

Speaking of the sick and the lame, I recall our Lord telling a story in which a rich man gave a great banquet. He invited the rich and the famous, the bright and the beautiful, but none accepted his generous invitation. Then the man of the house being angry said to his servant Go out quickly into the streets and lanes of the city, and bring in the poor and the maimed, the lame and the blind. "These we are told, humbly accepted. They ate and drank and danced to their hearts content and to the rich man's delight as well" (Luke 14:15–24).

Truly God's ways are far and high above our ways, thankfully we do not need to understand everything so to please Him, but only to believe Him on His own terms, no matter how obscure our reckoning of truth and justice may seem to be. Make no mistake, much about God can be known and much is yet to be fathomed, but till the end, there will be mystery. This is just what we should expect, where the Infinite meets the finite. That which remains mysterious is God's prerogative requiring trust on our part, which is most commonly called faith.

The following are quotes from a highly recommended book called *Mere Christianity* by C. S. Lewis, selected verses from pages 168 and 169.

Lewis says:

> "That was what people objected to about Christ during His life on earth: He seemed to attract such awful people. That is what people still object to and always will…"
>
> "They are the lost sheep: He came specially to find them…"
>
> "They are the awful set He goes about with…"
>
> "If you are a nice person—if virtue comes easily to you—beware! Much is expected from those whom much is given. If you mistake for your own merits, what are really God's gifts to you through nature?… You are still a rebel."
>
> But if you are a poor creature—poisoned by wretched upbringing in some house full of vulgar jealousies and senseless quarrels—saddled by no choice of your own, with some loathsome sexual perversion—nagged day in and day out by an inferiority complex that makes you

> snap at your best friend—do not despair:
> He knows all about it. You are one of the
> poor whom He blessed. He knows what a
> wretched machine you are trying to drive.
> Keep on. Do what you can. One day per-
> haps in another world, but perhaps far
> sooner than that) He will fling it no the
> crap-heap and give you a new one. And
> then you may astonish us all—not least
> yourself: For you have learned you're driv-
> ing in a hard school. (Some of the last will
> be first and some of first will be last).

No doubt, it is best to come to God early and often, but short time or long what is ultimately important is a quality relationship with Him. Again, no doubt many of us have come to God the long way around, and by this route, we may be well sounded in the depths of experience and learning, but this way is that hard school of which Mr. Lewis spoke.

A secular example of this process comes to mind in the life experience of the great "Wizard of Menlo Park," Mr. Thomas Edison. Once when Edison was being ridiculed and diminished by the press for having failed many hundreds of times before finally succeeding with his incandescent light bulb, he exclaimed, that he most certainly did not fail hundreds of times, but rather, that he discovered hundreds of ways that do not work. No doubt the way of Mr. Edison's discovery was hard, but thoroughly learned. Therefore, if you are anything like Mr. Edison, take courage, for it is often very dark before the "light" shines bright!

But remember above all, "forgivers will be forgiven." Now if we are forgiven we are God's own children who live unchained and in the light. I did not say we live perfect or sinless lives, but only that we live in the perpetual light of His gracious forgiveness.

> "For if you forgive men their trespasses (sins), your heavenly Farther will also forgive you. But If you do not forgive men their trespasses, neither will your Father forgive your trespasses." (Matt. 6:14–15)

> Then Peter came to Him (Jesus) and said, "Lord, how often shall my brother sin against me, and I forgive him? Up to seven times?" Jesus said to him. "I do not say to you, up to seven times, but up to seventy times seven." (Matt. 18:21–22)

> Incidentally, the number is not 490 times either, but rather an infinite number is implied.
> "I Jesus have sent My angel to testify to you these things in the churches. I am the root and the offspring of David, the Bright and Morning Star. And the Spirit and the Bride say, "Come"! And let him who hears say come. And let him who thirsts come. Whoever desires let him take the water of life freely." (Rev. 22:16–17)

Friends, we all suffer, everyone is misunderstood, and Jesus is our only perfect example of enduring these sorrows, but also of its solution, which is courage (like all good lions) and encouragement toward others (like lambs and shepherds).

> "Behold, I send you out as sheep in the midst of wolves.
> Therefore be wise as serpents and harmless as doves." (Matthew 10:46)

> "Let brotherly love continue." (Hebrew 13:11)

Friends,

Pray for our incarcerated brothers and sisters that they would understand...

"What seems to us bitter trials are often blessings in disguise." (Oscar Wilde)

Or "that some of us must be stopped in our errors so to finally come to know our Creator; that life is sacred and eternity bliss." (Me)

Ray Amato
May 2015
South Amboy, NJ

ON EVANGELISM

Driving south on City Line Avenue in the "City of Brotherly Love," I spotted a homeless man on the corner at a red light. Like the Old Spice sailor from a high perch, I felt compelled to toss him my pretty little pocket Bible. He looked at it and seemed to marvel with delight, perhaps because it was new and clean and holy—things maybe he is not used to. Well, don't ya know some days later while traveling the same route I spotted that same man on a park bench reading a little book with the intensity it seemed of a scholar. Who knows how well he can even read, but one thing I believe we may confidently expect is that if he be truly interested he has the best of teachers. The Spirit and The Word.

The Good News tells us that those who seek shall find, and we should also understand that God often enjoys calling and using common people, even lowly people to accomplish His best work, perhaps so that no one gets confused as to whose work it really is, like the fisherman and the tentmakers who were so honored as to record for us God's written revelation, no less than the greatest literary work this side of heaven.

Sometimes the supernatural invades the natural compelling us to move for the salvation of the lost. Question: Is that predestination, or should we call it election, or choice? Now that's a tangled enough web of worms to keep the theologians busy and out of trouble for a while. Haha! Anyway, it certainty is evangelism, a thing to which by God we are commissioned in a most Catholic fashion. Let no one think me antagonistic here, I mean in a most united and universal fashion, because that is the true meaning of the word Catholic and it is not a bad word.

I really think that many of our trans-denominational disputes are more offensive to God then the mistakes we assume others make in their interpretations. "Mercy triumphs over judgment," said our Lord, I mention this even though it may not seem to fit with my little story above, because it does fit. Good argument is good, but when it becomes angry, stubborn, and divisive it most surely weakens our testimony, as our ability and power depends on our oneness with God, which He seems to say is enhanced when the Church agrees, or at least when it agrees to disagree for unities sake and for Christ's sake. I do not include the plain imperatives of our common faith, for they are not obscure, but there are many gray areas and they must be gray by design, since our designing, omniscient God could have easily made us understand everything, but He hasn't.

We know that pride is at the root of all our sins, but when it finds itself like a cankerous worm in the heart of the living Church it does its most lethal damage nearly slamming in the face of the lost both the chapel and cathedral doors. In any event, we find solace in the fact that what doors God opens no man or demon may shut, but woe to those of us who cause unwarranted descent in the Church, in which case the thieves, drunkards and prostitutes may precede us through the Pearl Gates of the Celestial City.

We really do appear to God as very little children and that I think is why He unconditionally forgives all who call Jesus their Savior, because if we really were as smart as we sometimes like to think of ourselves, then God might not see us as little children, who as everyone knows are much more readily forgiven.

From the Sermon on the Mount our Lord spoke to those who would collectively soon be called the Church:

> "You are the light of the world. A city
> that is set on a hill cannot be hidden."
> (Matthew 5:14, NKJV)

I don't know about anyone but myself, so I will speak for myself. When I sin against God and especially against His Bride, that is the Church, I do not feel like a beacon on a hill, but more like a mere man of clay crouching and hiding in a garden.

> Then the Lord God called to Adam and
> said to him, "Where are you?" So he
> (Adam) said, "I heard your voice in the
> garden, and I was afraid because I was
> naked; and I hid myself." (Genesis 3:9–10)

Let me say it one final way and I am done:

Offend a man and if he be a temperate and reasonable man you may escape unscathed, but offend his bride and you will surely reap the whirlwind. This is natural with men as with God whose image and attributes we are created in the likeness of. If we think before maligning a strong mans beloved wife, perhaps we should think twice before maligning our all-powerful God's beloved Bride.

Unity on our common faith, which is Jesus Christ crucified for our sins, then raised from the dead will be the thing that promotes powerful evangelism and true revival in the Church universally all to God's glory, amen.

Ray Amato
Jan. 2016
So. Amboy, NJ

PATRIOTISM

In the 1776th year of our Lord, a select group of selfless and educated men, pious and patriotic men gathered in the City of Brotherly Love at the clear risk of a treasonous hanging for the crime of choosing freedom. Mr. Benjamin Franklin put it thus to his fellows, "We must all hang together," he said, "or we shall all hang separately." Willing to pay this potential price for the greater good these men crafted our nation's original governing documents, implemented by a declaration of independence, finally realized through a declaration of war. A war, not incidentally, waged against the greatest empire in the world of that day. Men from all thirteen original colonies congregated with little more than hunting rifles, willing to give their blood, sweat, and tears, even their lives so to bring victory to fruition. Those journeymen soldiers suffered in squalid and bitter cold winter camps, like at Morristown in North Jersey and the following winter west of the Schuylkill River at Valley Forge in Pennsylvania where nearly one-third of them perished, not at the hands of the Red Coats, but of those other enemies of war. As malnutrition, exposure, and disease took them. In the spring as the foliage pushed forth tender and green, so did they push forth, only no longer tender and green, but rather as a hardened force of seasoned veterans. They solemnly buried their buddies and brothers, their fathers and sons, then dutifully mustered the rest for the retaking of our then capital at Philadelphia, then pursuing the enemy double time across central Jersey on a sweltering hot day over 100 degrees and humid, finally engaging their main force in the bloody battle of Monmouth, where after a long and arduous fight the Brits decided that discretion was the better part of valor. Making their way to the sea in retreat they boarded ships for New York opting to fight another day. The tide of war was greatly turned on that unusually high-spirited day, as it seems in hindsight that God had big plans for this new nation!

The more wealthy men and women put up their fortunes and treasured estates to fund the effort, many of their men being educated became officers of rank, their women the strength of the fabric; God the how, us their children the why. Neither the rich nor the poor were ever repaid; nevertheless, they did not complain much, but rather with a patriotic industrialism mingled with faith they built a nation, by now the greatest nation on earth.

Fast forward 225 years to that other day, which shall live in infamy, September 11, 2001. On that day, I was working on a paint crew when one of the crew said, "I just heard on the radio that a large airliner has just crashed into the World Trade Center and it's on fire!" Big John replied, "What in the hell do you mean? Airliners don't accidentally crash into skyscrapers on a clear day and neither is their glide path over the skyline, it had to have been done purposely." Then after a pause he said, "They are here!"

Recalling the 1993 attack on the Trade Center. I thought for sure that he was right. Within minutes, the kid with his Walkman set reported the second crash, then later again, that one of the towers had fallen! I said to John, "So whose still mad at those Christian Crusaders of the middle ages maybe they'll get another hearing, for to be sure these terrorists are the sons of old—Jihadists." That's when we packed up our gear and solemnly headed home. I to Keyport, NJ, where I watched from my second story balcony some twenty miles (the way a gull flies) across the Raritan Bay. By then, the second tower had already fallen. The Twins were now just a smoldering heap, a mangle of twisted steel, concrete, and Christian martyrs. It is my fervent belief that God will someday resurrect those ashes of the faithful and no corruption shall ever again degrade them, nor will any consuming fire touch them.

While my experience was transpiring my brother Mark had a bird's eye-view of the horror watching from the pier in Jersey City as the first tower burned only three miles across the upper bay of NY harbor in lower Manhattan. He and the other drivers and dock workers watched in shocked silence as the second plane closed in on the second tower. I remember thinking as his dialogue unfolded that, that is a sight and experience that none of them on that pier that tragic summer morning shall ever forget, nor should we, as we also remember just exactly where we were when we received that sad and shocking news; the plight of thousands of our brothers and sisters in New York, NY, in Washington, DC, and in rural Sharksville, Pennsylvania.

It is now more than fifteen years later and this politicized war of attrition drags on and on, ebbing and flowing as patriotic soldiers are fed into the meat grinder, our leaders" (I use the word loosely) lacking resolve!

I now live in South Amboy, NJ also on the bay with an awesome view of that hulking statement, that spectacle, the Freedom Tower standing with perfect posture at 1,776 feet tall, one third of a mile high, watching out over "The New City" and vicinity. It is a rather blatant statement to those enemies of liberty, those evil butchers and cowards, those ____ Jihadists, and I trust the statement needs no interpretation, yet I offer one anyway. It is saying that we mourn profoundly, but we are not discouraged nor afraid; yet if we are to turn back such determined enemies, we will need leaders as brave and ready to act as those they assume to lead.

Let us pray now that we find the wisdom to choose the best leaders in these crucial coming elections. Faithful men and women who will lead our country with determination, discretion, humility, and a courageous patriotic loyalty, so that we may remain the truest beacon of hope this world has ever known. If not the saddest days may be yet to come. Yet we hope for better things so that the light which our "Lady of the Harbor" holds high may beam bright even so far as our friends in Europe where sadly the spiritual life has for some time been on the wane and with our nation not far behind.

Leaders lead, so let's get to it with faith, courage, and the spirit of our forefathers, those "Sons of Liberty" those 1776-ers. And finally we mustn't be fooled, it is our legal and God-given right to exercise our Judeo-Christian heritage. Remember those first American settlers crossed large dangerous oceans on small wooden ships for religious freedom, it is true that church and state should be kept separated as has been our practice, but this was meant to protect the church from state control. As a matter of fact, that was the very reason our forefathers and mothers, those pilgrims of old had set the sail, so to escape those theocracies of Europe. Separation of church and state was not meant to protect the state from the purifying effects of a faithful and virtuous people, the thing has been turned upon its head.

The direction for us now is to become an educated people, a praying, voting, hopeful people. After that only trust remains, which is most commonly called faith.

A QUESTION OF BALANCE
What Is Politics Like?

Politics is like two rival schools at a football game each rooting fanatically, almost slavishly for their own side. While this is acceptable even admirable at the Army and Navy game, it is neither helpful nor acceptable in Washington, DC, or in our state houses. If we are to be honest and reasonable, we will have to admit that it is natural even honorable that these should follow their own political bent whether liberal or conservative as this was the plan from the beginning of this democratic republic, as it brings checks, affording balance and this for the good of the greatest number. But far too often their objective is to appease those few who donate generously to their reelection campaigns or even fouler things then that and this occurs on both sides as predictably as those rival school boys and girls. These overwhelmingly partisan politicians should recognize that while they are rival fraternities they are at the same time members of the same school, that they are no longer school boys and girls so easily swayed by emotion and personal gain, but rather by now mature and fore thinking men and women. Again, everyone enjoys the rivalry at the Army and Navy game, for it brings out the best in both, but when it comes down to brass tacks. I mean for instance our national defense or bringing aid to a disaster area we can be assured that both the soldiers and the sailors will be of one accord for the greater good; not sabotaging one another for personal or collective gain or for recognition, but rather complimenting each other for our country and its good name.

As you know many bills that are brought to the floors of congress for vote come down strictly along party lines for fear that one side or the other will get credit for the progress that it might bring in our struggle to succeed. This is in many cases obviously disingenuous, for it is not possible that any bill presented could be at the same time a great idea and a terrible one, but this is the type of tripe they try to feed us when they play these sickening and unproductive partisan games, as this continual wresting in the miry trenches has produced a predictably monotonous and boring stalemate.

Perhaps term limits would help these men and women live up to their lofty titles, the honorable senator or representative of these fifty great United States.

Ray Amato
12-23-2009
Leesburg, NJ
Pulpit Prison Message

ENTER THROUGH THE NARROW GATE

Plainly stated, the reason we often do not sense the peace and security that should rightfully be ours as Christian is due to our carnality (the pursuit of our own pleasures, passions, and desires, in disregard of God's will.)

We were not designed to live strictly by natural instinct, as all other living things are. That is because man and man alone has been created in God's image.

Then God said (speaking within the trinity), "Let us make man in Our *image*, according to Our likeness; let them have dominion over the fish of the sea, over birds of the air, and over the cattle, over all the Earth and over every creeping thing that creeps on the Earth" (Genesis 1:26).

The cattle of the Great-Plains and of the African Savanna Congregate in Massive herds for security. Wild dogs assemble in packs, fish conform to great schools, birds gather in large flocks, even the insect world follows these principles. (The bees huddle among the hive and do battle in swarms) while the ant leads a productive life in his colony, but he suffers or perishes in solitude, as also does the lonewolf (the straggling fish, or the stray lamb.)

From the largest mammal to the smallest creeping insect, all follow God proscription by following each other in like kind and characteristics.

Natural men also tend to herd together in conformity to one another, like the common beasts. But this is Against God's design and description, man is to be a unique individual, a personality. Personality is the aspect that man alone possesses. This is what largely separates man from the animal kingdom. Personality is also the point at which man can be likened to the image of his Creator. Generic or natural man is common to the beast, in that, he lives according to his instincts or passions alone—rather than giving higher rule to God's will and authority. However the Christian tends to the common, mainly when he is out of step with the Holy Spirit; you *know, monkey* see, monkey do, you lie and steal, so do I. you get high, so do I, etc., and so on.

However, by the Holy Spirit's power Christians are no longer bound by that old sin nature. Sin may still live in our flesh but it does not have unrestrained rule. We are redeemed by the precious blood of God's own Son, and thereby, transcending the dictates of sin, we are becoming transformed, set apart, sanctified.

We are, says the Apostle, "a peculiar people, sanctified and set apart from the world." (That is to say, we are to jorney that narrow road less traveled.)

It is a mistake for Christians to adopt the worldview, the status quo, or the herd mentality. But in keeping balance, neither do we live autonomously, that is independent of Christ or His Church.

The worldly or natural man always seeking life in his own self-interest never finds life, even while he lives. Conversely, the humbled man being trained by God through diverse blessings and disciplines is alive, body and spirit. He is at peace while he lives in agreement with God's will and at long last his condition is made complete, perfect, and eternal, amen!

Many in the world think themselves safe and secure before God, because they measure up pretty well to others. The point they miss is being like or even better than others (in the sense of morality, generosity, and service) is not how one finds peace in life, nor eternal life. Life fully lives now and life eternal is a gift of God. It cannot be earned or bought at any price. It is by grace offered and by faith received.

For the man of the world, the insecurities of life and prospect of death, leave him unfulfilled and frankly scared. In quest of peace, he may make some superficial claim of faith. "But faith without works," says James, "is dead." Equally as vain, is works without faith. Either extreme is at bottom a self-imposed, self-seeking effort, not a God-directed one. In trying to find themselves worthy of God's blessings—they compare themselves to others in the world (while conveniently dismissing true Christians as Jesus freaks or hypocrites).

"When you compare yourselves among yourselves," says St. Paul the Apostle, "you are unwise. Rather compare yourselves to God."

The once-born or worldly man may attain wealth and fame, but he must in the passing of time decline, die, and face certain judgment.

The believer, on the other hand being, twice born that is, born physically and spiritually also declines and physically dies, but his soul is saved—his spirit eternal, the born-again man travels from life to life...

The point Paul is making is this, when we compare ourselves to God's perfect standard, that is, His Word or His Christ, we do not get discouraged because we have a Savior, but we do recognize our imperfections and our need of that Savior.

It accounts for little if the world calls me a good follow, because, their judgments are only relative to other men who change to whatever happens to be in vogue at the time. That which was not morally acceptable yesterday, may be so today. What really does matter is what God thinks and says concerning man, according to His standard. His standard is His very own character, which does not change.

A few quick examples of the flexing and fickle, changing worldview.

Up until the 1950s, a man and a woman who could not produce a marriage certificate could not legally rent a room. Now a man may marry another man and together they may adopt children, with the world's full congratulations.

In around the 1940s, movie star Clark Gable, in one of his lines of the classic movie, *Gone with the Wind*, said, "Frankly I don't give a damn." WOW, the people of America were in shock that anyone would dare say "damn" on the big screen. Compare that with what we see and hear on TV and in movies today. Same God, very different and benumbing worldview.

Again, only since 1973, abortion was illegal, and by many considered murder of the most innocent. Now it is considered a right of liberty. But what about the liberty, we might ask of the nearly fifty million exterminated babies since. By the way, fifty million is eight times as many victims as were killed in Hitler's holocaust. Adolf Hitler, the most notorious anti-Christ, of the most blood century in history.

But this modern-day holocaust, this mass murder is not committed by an evil dictator, but by the hands of the victims' own parents and their doctors. Yet the world finds no occassion for shock.

Then there is what formerly was my favorite sin—drug and alcohol abuse, including the many other various ills that it brings about to the ruin of the addict, his family and the degrading of society all around.

For sure, these problems always existed, but they have adversely affected our communities to new and overwhelming extremes, especially in these past few decades under our watch and guard.

Turn to Isaiah chapter 24: Here Isaiah is speaking to the Israel of his day, but the prophet also speaks to our generation.

"The Earth mourns and fades away, the world languishes and fades away; the naughty people of the Earth *languish (weaken, become weary and unsetteled)*."

"The Earth is also defiled under its inhabitants, because they have transgressed the law, changes the ordinance, broken the everlasting covenant" (Isaiah 24:4–5).

The most key phrase here pertaining to our topic is "The Earth is defiled because they have changes the ordinance." Changed the ordinance, means changes God's laws of decree—as you can plainly see is the case.

Israel was trying to lower God's standards to suit themselves, much as the world is doing today. One can try all he likes, but God's judgment is for those who do so (and double for those who mislead others. Judgment, for the individual first, but also of the nation whose ordinances contradict God's).

In Matthew 7:13–14, Jesus is speaking.

"Enter by the narrow gate; for wide is the gate and broad is the way that leads to distruction, and there are many who go in by it."

"Because narrow is the gate and difficult is the way which leads to life, and there are few who find it."

Brothers, Jesus is the Gate, and crucifixion is the way. This sounds extreme because it is. It is at times an extreme and arduous way of life, but it is not at all an extravagant calling when compared to the reward or compared—God forbid to its alternative.

Many people who will go to the greatest extremes to gain temporary wealth are often the same who find God's standard of holiness an extravagant request, even in view of a treasure without limit in quantity, quality, or duration. Isn't it right to say that such an attitude implies either a lack of understanding or, even worse, a lack of faith, for it must be one or the other (unless it is, purposefully, disobedient, rejection of God, which is characteristic of the dreaded anti-Christ spirit).

Scripture tells us, "Though we must live in this world, we are not to be of this world."

And Peter writes, "We are strangers in this world, that our citizenship is in heaven." And so heaven's higher law must be our governor.

Resisting the worlds or herd mentality may be met with disdain, persecution, and alienation. But by the security and peace, which is ours in reward of obedience, we not only can endure hardship but also we our assured victory over death, a guarantee through the merits of Jesus Christ our Lord and faithful Shepherd who leads us through that narrow way into the green pleasant fields of the New Jerusalem, amen!

Brothers, with a God so great having created the universe by divine fiat, so personal, He calls us children, giving each of us life and personality so to commune with Him. So loving as to send His only begotten Son to die, so we might live; with these in mind, the Apostle asks, "What type of people ought we to be?" Shouldn't we be grateful people, happy people, confident and content people? People of praise?

But we can only be grateful, confident people of praise, if we know God personally.

Yes. Words can tell us these things, but only He can manifest in us their reality. The praise then comes naturally and unforced in this process. And it is heightened all the more by increasing obedience. Its result is song and all kind of gifts to the edification of the Church, which in turn glorifies God, which is our ultimate goal.

Someone once asked, "What is man's purpose in life?" Giving this question full consideration, the Westminster Church of England gave its answer, short and sweet. "Man's purpose," they said, "is to glorify God and enjoy Him forever."

To know God we need to know what He said, read and study the Bible. And James 1:22 says, "But be doer of the word, and not hearers only; deceiving yourselves."

We need to hear the truth, and confess our faith. We must acknowledge our sins with a contrite and repentant heart. Then we must be willing to carry our cross, which is not a herd or group activity, but a sometimes lonely one.

An impossible task for a mere man, you say? True enough, but Jesus said, what is impossible for man alone is possible with God. With His Holy Spirit as the source of power, patience, and heavenly protocol.

By salvation in Jesus Christ, which is made more sure and spiritually sensible by obedience to His Word and will, our peace in this life and our hope of eternal life is more than hope, it is already ours. We will enter through the narrow Gate as we follow our God Shepherd.

AMEN!

SUNDAY CHAPEL MESSAGE (BAYSIDE STATE PRISON)

In our predominantly Christian, western world, speaking mainly of the countries of Europe and the Americas, men have been *free*, even encouraged to worship God. However, the name of Christ has sounded very shallow waters in these last days. New Testament doctrine clearly deems such shallow faith as lukewarmness and dangerously close to no faith at all. I'm sorry to say lukewarmness describes the condition of most of my own life and much of the church as well. This is a colossal oversight in the church. Today people are lulled to sleep in the arms of mother church, the sleeping giant herself.

In the book of Revelation, the Apostle John shows Israel in a similarly wanting light, when he refers to her as Sodom and Egypt, that is abominable, immoral and pagan, in need of repentance. Pagan not in the sense of stone image worship but in lust of things, false pride, self-worship!

By the year 70 AD, the Israelites were expelled from their beloved homeland. Those who rejected and crucified their Massiah had themselves died on Roman crosses and of disease and starvation. But in the Old Testament, God promised to always preserve a remnant of Israel. With evil in hot pursuit, a remnant of course did escape into many parts of the world. This was predicted by the prophet Zachariah as follows: "When I strike the Shepherd the sheep will be scattered" (Zachariah 13:7). Also the Jews have never been genuinely accepted in any nation in which they tried to settle. They had been rejected, hated, and brutally purged for 1,900 years. Today all surrounding nations want Israel dead, just like the devil. Why all this suffering? Israel was given the best of the land, the Word of God, prophets to guide them in the ways of salvation. A book should be written on this subject not a sentence. But let me try it in one sentence. To whom much is given, much is expected. Now the same is true for us, because we too are sons of Abraham by adoption. Here's the good news for Israel. The Apostle Paul says, "And so all Israel will be saved as it is written" (Rom. 11:26).

Israel will be saved, whether Jew or Gentile. But this never comes without pain as we can all attest. This is because all men are born with a rebellious nature. To some extent, all are rebels against God and all rebels must be broken. Like the wild horse who receives no rider, or pulls no wagon but must first be broken or else be useless to his master.

Proverbs says, "God disciplines us as a father does to the son he delights in."

Concerning salvation, God is always previous. That is, as the scriptures make clear he loved us and called us first. But it is for us to receive his training even though it is converse to our nature. Sin and rebellion cause suffering, so suffering precedes are salvation so to draw us, then continues so to keep us and grow us. A vine that is not pruned will never be profitable to the vine dresser. The scriptures also tell us that obedience is what causes the Holy Spirit to burn bright in our heart. That is to say, the love and acceptance of God poured in on our spirit is our confidence that we are saved eternal sons. And the growth of the persecuted churches of the east and the stagnation of the pampered churches of the West serve as our best evidence that the church or the man that gallantly carries his cross is the most blessed with such assurance of belonging to God.

"Consider it pure joy my brothers whenever you face trials of many kinds, because you know that the testing of your faith develops perseverance. Perseverance must finish its work so that you may be mature and complete, not lacking anything" (James 1:2–4). When is God's work of sculpting our characters finished, when are we completed? I think not until we die or rather are transformed into his likeness. And what does the Apostle say, "I do not consider this present suffering comparable to the peace and joy of our eternal reward." And I might add that this peace that we experience now as committed believers far exceeds the false and illusive peace that we formerly pursued.

It is in this common course of human suffering that we attempt to persuade others to also and finally abandon the false pride of self-worship and except the free gift of life offered to all who grant God, his due worship and acknowledge his Lordship over all of heaven and earth which he created, maintains, and holds all authority over, and all rights of blessing or judgment.

Ni Shu Tsu, Watchman Nee, a Christian leader and author in China asks a question. "What happens when people submit to the work of the Lord in reshaping their lives? This is what happens," says Nee, "the lazy become diligent, the talkative become quiet, the selfish become selfless, and the prideful become humble. Those fearful of suffering develop a mind to suffer, and the uncontrolled become disciplined. The weak become strong, and those who previously were ever busy in the ways of this world are caught up with the ways of the world to come."

Short Story Section

In The Mix Of A New England Nor'eastern

This trip was logged December 23 and 24. I remember not what year, save that it was during the mid-1980s. My rig was parked out back behind our apartment, loaded with ten Honda automobiles. Destination: five cities in the great state of Maine. Christmas was only a few days away, so I needed to pull out in the wee hours next morning if I were to be home for that hallowed day. I kissed my wife and two little girls good night early that evening and got underway about 3:30 a.m. so that I could make my final drop that night nearly seven hundred loaded miles.

According to plan, I skirted by Hartford, Connecticut, just before the morning rush, then by noon made Kiltery, Maine, at the southern state line, taking on fuel and some lunch. I had been hearing some ominous weather reports about an imminent nor'eastern, so there was little time to waste. It's about another hours travel to my first stop at Falmouth, Maine, just north of Portland, then Auburn, next off at the state Capitol at Augusta then Bangor 130 miles farther on which was accomplished by late afternoon.

Now it's another 160 miles to my fifth and final stop at Presque Isle very near the top of the Boot. In fact, Maine is so long north to south (especially when compared to the typically smaller state surrounding her) that when you reach her southern state line starting from New Jersey you are only halfway to Presque Isle. Interstate 95 runs out at Houlton, Maine, on the east Canadian border at the Province of New Brunswick, then it's a left due north fifty more miles on route one also called by New Englanders "The Old Post Road" mostly hill country through that region embroidered by endless potato fields. It was so cold that my heater provided only cool air even at continuous full throttle, then the snow began to fall.

When I rolled into town, the flashing bank sign told the tale, it was after 7:00 p.m. and six degrees below zero. I have experienced extremely cold weather before, and since, like when loading Cadillacs in Dearborn, Michigan, or Chryslers in Buffalo, NY, or Buicks in the Windy City, but never anything quite like this. With gale force winds blowing in off the North Atlantic, the radio called the windchill factor in a sixty odd below zero. Thus the sales manager warned, "You better hunker down in town tonight 'cause it's gonna be a bad one." Dave's gray crown suggested he might know a few things about Maine's wintery episodes, so I heeded his advice: "No question about it, Dave," I said. "I'm tired and cold as hell anyway."

At the hotel, I parked facing downhill to get a running start out of what promised to be a deep coat of snow by morning. In the a.m., before dawn, I drank a strong black cup then headed out against better judgment, since it was a white-out blizzard in progress with about eighteen inches already on the ground and drifts too many feet against structures. It was early in my career so I didn't realize how limited the plow crews were in those remote parts of God's country; in fact, I didn't see a single snow plow for more than a hundred miles, but even if they had plowed Route 1, the gale winds blowing across barren potato fields would have quickly erased their work. I really shouldn't have pulled out so early, but as I said, the family was expecting me home that night. Being empty made things all the worse, but seeing that an empty car carrier trailer is still pretty heavy and that at only about eight inches off the ground its belly would surely take on weight as the bottom decks filled with packed snow.

So off we go, keep it screamin' and hope you don't have to stop or there you may have to stay. Visibility was so poor that one could hardly tell if he were on Route 1 or on a potato field. Thank God for the dark shadows of telephone poles, which were the only decipherable guide. The fifty miles to Houlton took more than two hours and don't ya know by then those old boys at the Houlton dinner with their plaid coats and hats with ear flaps had that antique Norman Rockwell lookin' dinner parkin' lot shaved clean, beckoning weary travelers in, which would have been a no-brainer had there been any travelers, but apparently, they did have a brain and stayed home. They said I was one of only a few trucks they had seen thus far that morning. Then one asked me if I was a little crazy, a thing that I could not thoroughly deny. "Isn't that a single screw tractor?" he asked.

"Yep," I replied as they just shook their heads. Single screw means that only one axle of the tractor is a drive axle, the other is just a dummy for carrying weight. After coffee and a quick bite, off I went. "Better say your prayers, son," one said.

"Always do," I replied. "And anyway God always looks out for drunks and fools, so I'm doubly protected, don't ya know," to which they laughed heartily. Immediately out of the diner lot came the northern most gate of that east coast Interstate 95. To my surprise and dismay, not even 95 showed any evidence of plow activity as the snow reached the two-foot mark through now-warming air, causing the snow to become sticky and heavier. It's about 120 miles from Houlton to the next vestige of considerable population at the City of Bangor. It wasn't but a few miles into this leg of the trip when my passenger's side windshield wiper (which had become heavy with ice) had fallen off. This didn't overly concern me, but within only a few more miles, the driver's side wiper flopped off. Now that's a problem, 'cause again, it's still whiteout conditions and unplowed. I was forced to slow way down to about the fourth gear out of ten as visibility became nearly nil. Just then, as hope seemed to wane, I heard over the CB radio, "What's wrong portable parkin' lot ya brakin' down?"

"Not exactly," I said. "Both my wipers fell off and I can't see a thing, but nor can I stop 'cause I'm dragin' and if I stop that's where I'll stay. Do you think you can get through that snow drift they call a left lane?"

"Sure, I can, my friend, I've got a four and a quarter Cat with twin screws pullin'," he replied. When he pulled out into the left lanes, three-foot snow draft all I saw was black smoke pouring from his stacks and an explosion of white powder totally obscuring him from vision (quite a romantic moment in hindsight at least as a road man sees it), then he appeared again as he came even with me. This guy was good, cool as a cucumber as they say. I shall never forget as he went by he grinned at me with a toothpick in his mouth like "Jim Croce's Rapid Roy that stock-car boy," who was as Jim said, "too much to believe." When his trailer finally cleared, I flashed him over so that I could follow his flashers red glow through the slush on my windshield. He escorted me nearly one hundred miles in that fashion (even though I slowed him down considerably) till I reached the Bangor-Brewer truck stop for repair. "Hey, what's your handle tanker?" I asked.

"Angel," he said.

"All right, Angel. Mine's Lonewolf," I replied kind of sheepishly. As I finally pulled off that exit, I again thanked him for his graciousness. "All right, Lonewolf," he said. "Now you be careful 'cause it's 350 mountain miles till you reach New Haven on the coast then you can coast on down to that Raritan Bay in the great Garden State."

"I know you're right, Angel. Hey what's your government name?" I asked.

Keying up his mic, he said, "Gabe."

"Ya mean as in Gabriel?" I prodded.

"Yep, that's right," he replied.

"That's an appropriate name for an angel," I jested, as he disappeared into the mist of eighteen wheels on the now-heavy wet slush. Wait a minute, I don't remember telling him that I lived on the Raritan Bay. In any event, I reached my home safely, a little later than expected, but long before old St. Nick arrived with his payload.

Author's Note

This story is firmly based in truth except for the insinuation that the other driver was perhaps a real angel, but then again, who knows. For in truth, God looks after drunks and fools and everyone else, and moreover, that we are watched over by angels, I for one do testify in the affirmative and for many more reasons than this one.

The severity of the above trip turns out as a blessing. First because it was awesome, eventful, and beautiful and secondly because such occasions as these will forever be retained in one's memory. I mean, if I had instead that day picked a southern or western trip, it would have long ago been lost in a blur of commonality and if my spirit were low, even monotony.

Incidentally, in spite of popular folklore, wolves are extremely noble creatures, even when left alone, a thing that does not come easily to men; therefore, it must be considered a gift strictly beyond boasting, unless of course ones boast is in the LORD, whose host of angels serve anonymously at His good pleasure.

R. Amato
Oct. 2000
Belmar, NJ

DONNY'S SONG

I remember my friend Donny,
we met just months before he died.
He showed me pictures of his family;
his children and his bride.
When Donny cried, "Cocaine's my god,"
I knew that he was lying,
Rather, he was bitter toward the virus
by which he was dying.
By the time I first met my friend
he was mostly wasted away,
He hadn't left that drug-infested welfare hotel
forever and a day.
Donny had been a billiards shark, well anyway,
that is what he said,
But by now he couldn't even walk downstairs
so I carried him instead.
At the pub he had trouble shooting pool,
he could hardly stand or see.
It's touching as I recall his slight smile
Donny had found a friend in me.
During Donny's final weeks bitterness and fear
queerly subsided.

Between drugs, the devil and the deep blue sea,
I told him of free asylum—"Amazing Grace!"
It was then my friend found refuge
in Christ his Savior!
Like everyone, I too loathe the thought
of mingling drugs and evangelism
But there was no time, for just then
I could not quit,
Nor was any other, in that place
found or fit.
Donny never called me a hypocrite, though,
perhaps fearing I'd go away,
For if I were to leave him alone,
who would be left to say,
"Donny, Jesus died in your place,
for your sins you need not pay."
Surely many well-meaning people
were in their fine cathedrals
encouraging one another,
However, none could be found that day so to encourage
me or my brother…
No doubt wisdom is proved right in time
when she says such,
"He who is forgiven a lot
is likely to love much."
So Donny forgave my inadequacy
as forgiveness is truly the key,
For it is to the degree that you judge others
that God will indeed judge ye.
Upon my arrival at that house one day, China Girl

greeted me with tears and said,
"I'm so sorry, but Donny died this morning,
he said to tell you,
he will see you again
on the other side,
where sinners are welcome by grace,
but self-righteous hypocrites denied."
No doubt, many of us have been kicked
and many drugged around.
But as of late none have been seen
dragging his cross through town;
So take courage in the time which remains,
for this is God's good pleasure;
Fly like eagles and be very courageous
while you still can,
Till He carries us then, when,
for ourselves we cannot fend.

Like that other "House of the Rising Sun," Donny's
final earthly,
home the "Sterling Hotel" stood on Ocean Ave.
across from
historic "Convention Hall" at the boardwalk in
Asbury Park, NJ.
His new eternal home is infinitely better and so is
his health, Amen!

Behind the wall, BSP
Leesburg, NJ

TSUNAMI SORROW
OF SOUTHEAST ASIA

It was nearly Christmas in the 2004th year of our Lord,
when under bright sunny skies the earth suddenly con-
vulses, quaking with ultra-enormous force out deep off the
island shore of Sumatra. Shock waves from the low beds
of the Indian Ocean are detected near and far. The earth's
covert sandy desert dunes perfectly disguised beneath two
miles of water, cracks, belches, and heaves. Only a relative
ripple in this vast pond is a killer in the distant islands and
as far west as the African coast. Hundreds of thousands are
soon to perish, entire villages erased, islands wholly inun-
dated with seawater, debris and with bodies strewn or else
dragged out to sea.

A single clairvoyant insight of a mega traumatic event
can touch us more than the death of its anonymous masses.
Such was the case for the writer as the plight of a single
soul was indelibly burned into my heart and mind more
readily than a quarter million ever could. Predictably, as
the tidal wave approached the surf suddenly receded hundreds of feet, it was a marvelous sight to a child on the
beach. Instead of running for high ground, he with child-
ish curiosity descended the grade, perhaps to investigate
some marooned fish flapping and glistening under the sun,

little knowing that this instant low-tide phenomenon is a sure sign of an eminent tsunami.

A tourist's camera viewing the scene from a hotel balcony captured this painfully touching event: a little boy about four or five with long swimming trunks reaching past his knees happily hastens to the sight of fish and shells with laughter and excitement, but shortly and again, he is pictured in a frozen pose as he finally notices the hulking wall of water approaching, it's thunderous violence squelches out the boy's feeble cry for mother. As the tumultuous churn of sand and seawater crash and tumble toward him laughter and delight give way to tears of frozen fright as the little one is swallowed by the monster.

Forgive me for breaking your heart; however, it has its purpose. This exceedingly sad and unforgettable tragedy engraved in the mind's eye begs one to embrace the pain and sorrow of others, which I believe is so very important to Christian living, but really, it is of vital importance to all humanity because it's yield is a boat load of compassion nurturing love universally in the brotherhood of man, it is even the crucible in which religion is refined and proved real—really. But woe to be God who perfectly understands the myriad details of all those who lost loved ones that fateful day, now add to that colossal loss all other suffering worldwide, including animal suffering. I believe that if God unveiled to us the full weight of all sorrow occurring on earth at any given time, as He experiences it, it would crush us so thoroughly as to die of an instant broken heart, but what if we felt no sorrow? Is not sorrow an indispensable source of love to be in some strange way embraced?

"Blessed are the poor in spirit, those that mourn, for they shall be comforted," spoken by Jesus at The Sermon on the Mount.

This work is dedicated to that little boy on the beach. I must thank him someday in heaven (where all things are corrected) for the revelation I received through his family's loss. For in reality of eternity, that innocent baby boy lost nothing.

On a personal note, I must say that the sorrow I have felt for others and even myself especially during twenty years of addiction and profound loss that such has in some way kept me connected to God in Christ. This begins to explain my strange affair with the emotion of sorrow as it occurs in real life and in art. For without it, I would have had to endure suffering without "blessed sorrow," which must surely be the reality of spiritual death, which would, of course, be the most tragic of all events.

Ray Amato
From the Caddy Shack at Mountclair Golf Club, 1997

GRACEFUL HAWK!
GRACEFUL PEOPLE?

High above Eagle Rock Gorge
I saw a hawk on glide mode:
he did not flap, nay, nor even flutter a wing.
Being in fact well founded in faith
he discovered effortless flight
upon the winds of change gladly.
He seemed content to me and why not
for he was everything a hawk could be;
he is what he is by grace, but so are we.

We may think life is not as it should be, but not so the graceful hawk. Satisfied to be what and where we are, when and
as we are, taking life's charms and troubles both with grace is
masterly, but balking and sulking is contemptuous of God,
which weighs heavily. By resisting life on life's terms, we do
not cease to be part of God's predestined order; however,
we certainly will not achieve the heights of its contentment
and confidences. To soar in the heights of God's reality, our
spirits must be lightened—that is, liberated from the bonds
of doubt and fear, which are diametrically opposed to faith
and courage, then we can soar gladly in any calm or storm;

we can be appreciative in a palace or content in a prison. In this hope abounds as life in reality is fully lived, as surely as we are in Christ fully and eternally alive.

> Truly, if the hawk can so gracefully do,
> so can I, and
> so can you,
> Amen?

The above scene occurred in West Orange, NJ, from Eagle Rock Mountain's heights, but I wrote it out just down the road while sitting in the caddy shack waiting for my next "loop" or should I say, my next "glide" around the magnificent and gorgeously groomed circa 1880s Montclair Golf Club with its stately mahogany clubhouse, a clubhouse incidentally which I had formerly been permitted to enter back in 1978 when I was a golf professional there. Now one must admit, it would seem to require some measure of grace to be a lowly content caddy there some fifteen years later. Ahhh, but to whistle Dixie while walking long in a cold rain: well that "seems" quite another matter. I think even the hawk may frown on those days, even though he can fly.

8-13-2019
OCJ
Toms River, NJ

A SOUTHERN TOUR

Over twenty years ago, in the early 1990s, I happened to visit two very different churches located in the vicinity of Lake Marion, at Santee, South Carolina. As a tractor trailer driver in those days, I was carrying a load of nine Jaguars from my home terminal in Port Newark, New Jersey, to Coral Cables, Florida. Coral Cables is an old, quaint Floridian town located south of Miami near the tip of the mainland just before entering upon the Keys. On the way down, I took a hotel room at about the halfway point, which is midway through South Carolina just off I-95. It was a Saturday night so I looked in an area directory for a local church that I might attend. The next morning in my eighty-thousand-pound taxi, I drove to the church, parked on the shoulder of the state highway, and went in. The church was filled to the gills, but to my surprise, mine was the only white face among two hundred or so. The people were very friendly, and as I recall, the praise and preaching were fine indeed. After service, I was invited to stay for coffee and fellowship in the church basement, which I did with glad appreciation.

Work was slow back at our home port but busy in the ports of Miami and Brunswick, Georgia. So after making my delivery, I opted to shuttle a few loads up and down the Sunshine State between the two ports. At the end of the week, Brunswick loaded me in the direction of home. As I recall it was a peddlers load split all over the where, from Elizabethtown and Jacksonville in North Carolina, about nine ways to the tidewater towns of Norfolk, Virginia Beach, and Newport News with the final stop at Delaware's Capital at Dover, finally to rattle on home as our Honda ship had by now made port.

Well, don't ya know, on the way back up north I got tired again around that sleepy, swampy, Santee, SC, and rented a room again on a Saturday night. I enjoyed visiting different churches all over the thirty-five-state territory in which I roamed. So I picked a different church not far from the one I attended the week before. The next morning, I drove again to church, loaded this time with ten Dodge Colts. Upon reaching this church and going in, I found it similar in size and decor, but opposite ethnically. This church was populated by all white people even though it was but a few miles from that all black church. Same as the week before the people were friendly the singing and preaching outstanding. After service came fellowship hour as seems to be the custom in the notoriously friendly south. During fellowship hour, the pastor asked me back to his home for Sunday dinner with his family. Of course like most any other lonesome cowboy hungry for a home-cooked meal, I accepted his kind and generous invitation.

The preacher's youngest child was a boy about nine years old. Upon leaving the sanctuary, the boy spotted my rig and replied in that familiar southern drawl, something like, "Wow, Dad, look at that." Remembering my first ride in my dad's rig many years before, I asked the boy if he would like to ride with me back to his house. "Of course I would, sir," he said with a delighted Tom Sawyer-lookin' grin or was it Huckleberry Finn.

While the girls were busy preparing dinner, the pastor and I talked shop in his study. I had been a Bible student for many years by then, with thousands of hours logged listening to the Bible on cassette tapes, as well as various teachings—so much so, that by this time, I could some-what keep up with a seminary trained man on many sub-jects including ecclesiastical ones, which was probably what really got his wheels turning.

In the past when people have inquired which Bible col-lege I went to, I have sometimes kiddingly told them, "The GMC Institute." Then when that searching look came over their face, I would say General Motors Corporation. If they still looked confused I would admit plainly, "No school, just my truck" but with the best of teachers, The Holy Spirit.

Anyway, the pastor and I were going along quite ami-ably talking about Christian doctrine, church history, and such, then for some reason beyond me, I plainly asked him, "How come there are no black people in your church?" I continued by explaining my previous weeks experience in that strictly black church. The question seemed almost involuntary, and it may have been in a way, because such a question would seem a bit too bold, even for me. Especially since I was an invited guest in the man's home. As I recall, I somewhat sheepishly began to apologize when he stopped me. "No," he said with his head down, "I know what you mean."

I remember thinking during dinner how neither the folks nor the pastors in either church seemed the slightest bit prejudice. It's just the way things had always been from our early colonial days of slavery clear through to the 1960s and Dr. King's civil rights movement and apparently to the present, but I had a strange feeling some change might soon be forthcoming in this local region.

After dinner, as time came to leave, I said my goodbyes and thanks-yous, then the pastor, whose name I'm sorry I don't recall, walked me to my truck. As we shook hands after he prayed for my safe journey, he looked me in the eye and asked me (if you can believe it) if I was an angel. Looking steady into his eyes, I believed him to be 100 percent sincere. Instead of laughing I only smiled slightly not wanting to insult his kind and respectful intentions, then, so to qualify his supposition he quoted from the Bible, Hebrew 13:1–2. "Let brotherly love continue. Do not forget to entertain strangers, for by so doing some have unwittingly entertained angels." Then he further embarrassed me by saying, "And angels you know, when they take on human form are often very attractive beings." As he made yet another guess, which also seemed highly doubtful, well I didn't know what to say except that I wasn't, but he looked at me as if to say, of course you can't admit it. I said "goodbye" and drove off quite touched by the whole affair, and I don't mind saying I still am to this day when I remember the time and the place and the people.

Some years later, it occurred to me that maybe in a figurative way, I was an angel. No, no, and a third time No, not one with wings and a halo and certainly not one of unimpeachable character. However, in the sense that the word *angel* means messenger and that I did bring a sharp and pointed message, which I myself could not account for or believe what I had actually uttered. Add to that his fallen face after I said it as though God had recently revealed to him in so many words the same. Maybe he was meant to think just what he thought.

What might happen if he confronts that other pastor saying, I believe I was visited by a heavenly messenger in a tractor trailer. Might not that pastor recall my visit to his church the week prior and perhaps also be energized toward change. Not that the two churches should necessarily integrate, but that they might interact in mutual fellowship as is so suited to their customs of southern hospitality. Who knows?

"But he (Beor) was rebuked for his iniquity: a dumb donkey speaking with a man's voice restrained the madness of the prophet." (2 Peter 2:16)

Again I say, who knows, if God once used a dumb jackass to correct a prophet, surely he could use a not so swift truck driver, if he chose to.

R. Amato
Jan. 2016
From the Pondarosa

VISIONS THROUGH THE VEIL

God does sometimes allow us glimpses into His mysterious realm, but only through a veil it seems. Not even the great Moses could look upon God's unveiled face: For God is how do they say all too too, to say the least, and please do not mistake my words as flippant in this regard, but rather and without batting an eye quite serious. For I can assure you of this one thing, "God is great," and at least at this point the "Saracens"[40] have got Him figured.

Anyway, sometime around the late nineteen nineties, I happened to be dragging a proverbial steel bridge loaded with nine Jaguar automobiles across the Ozark mountains of Arkansas on a hot and glary summer morn. As was typical with me, I had been listening to the Bible on audio tape for a long period; long enough in fact to put me half asleep when all of a sudden a strange thought occurred to me: "I'd love to see the might of God in a fierce storm," but it was sunny and fair all along the pleasant peaks as the thought left me to a simpler and calmer musing. A little later or as they say, down the road a piece I drifted off again, this time my mind was drawn to the solemn majesty of God's covenantel rainbow, many of which I have been privileged

---

[40] Followers of Mohammed.

to see all along my travels whether in suburbia USA, or in the big sky country of the great plains, or while cresting a ridge as the suns light shows it true colors in full spectrum through the prism of a sun shower.

Incidentally, once upon a time, high in the White Mountains of New Hampshire, I saw four rainbows simultaneously over four lower valleys, though I admit one was rather faint. Perhaps the three bright ones represent our triune God and the faint one us, so now do you see what I mean by the lingering veil?

Anyway back in the Ozarks, the dreamy miles were melting away as I found myself descending the western foothills of the Ozark range west-bound and down toward my two destinations at Tulsa and Oklahoma City, that's when the weather quickly began to deteriorate.

I had no clue what was coming since I was on the tapes all morning. The western sky turned an ominous purple black; it was awesome, in fact, we might finally and for once make use of that over used word "amazing" in its proper context, but I digress.

It was just about then that the tape player was shut off and the CB radio turned on. "Hey, how 'bout that westbound flatbed, you got a copy," I said.

"Yeah, go head parkin' lot," he replied.

So I asked, "What in the hell is that on our front door?"

"It's a son of a dog an' bastard super cell," he replied. "They been talkin' bout it all day on the FM, what you been doin' all day, sleepin'?"

Being an honest-to-goodness Christian cowboy, all I could say was, "Yep, pretty much," so he left it at that, not wishing to play the hypocrite, I suspect. As we gained on the storm, I noticed that most of the cars and empty trucks had pulled over on the shoulder or under overpasses all along the way, while the rest of us who were (in our own opinion) loaded heavily enough elected to proceed; hammer down, like a wild bend of gypsies, but only single file in the left lane so to leave room for those sidelined, safety first sojourners. Further into the storm, we could muster only about 40 mph as we were heading directly into the teeth of its hurricane force west wind. The driving rain was horizontal as were flying pieces of trees and the barometric pressure dropped so severely and quickly that our eardrums ached. Per usual, my air-conditioner was on the blink, so I had little choice but to leave my window open a crack on account of a screamin' Detroit Diesel stokin' a hellish environment within. Poor vision got the worse as rain water was quickly swept across the entire inside of my windshield and the whistling screech was deafening. The saga continued to mount as straight ahead a mile wide funnel cloud was coming right for us straight down Interstate 40, just a groovin' on a formerly sunny afternoon. As we entered the monster, our windshield wipers lilted up off the glass, still rotating but slightly in midair. I might have left this last part out thinking you might find it hard to believe, it certainty riddled me at the time, however, you may have in recent years seen that BMW car commercial where they brag of their new innovation in wiper technology, how theirs will remain on the glass well beyond that of their competition. If I recall the wind speed which causes wipers to blow up off the glass was approximately 150 MPM. Like I earlier said, we were traveling about 40 MPH, which means the head wind must have been at least 110 MPH, but I think it may have been greater.

As we entered the dismal haze of that whirlwind the veil in my mind was rent once more as I recalled that first daydream; I'd love to see the might of God in a fierce storm. Then I marveled. It seems that we may be at times semi clairvoyant, but most times, it seems, when partially conscious, somewhere in the mystic, which suggests yet another thing, that it's not necessarily us alone who initiates the communication.

But the half has yet to be told, if you recall I also daydreamed in an arched ribbon of colors. Yes, the rainbow too was brought to bear so bright and beautifully colored in the eastern sky as we viewed it in our west coast mirrors now looking back from the other side of the storm. That particular rainbow was the clearest and most vividly colored one I had ever seen owing probably to that deep purple black back drop. It seems that God does sometimes give us special clues of His near presence, but I think mostly when we're thinking of Him, even as it occurs in that sleepy veil called contemplation or meditation; it is that mystical place somewhere between here and there.

True enough, many people will stop when they see a storm on the horizon and I ain't mad at 'em, but others are more inclined to ride it out. As it turns out, I wasn't really in as much of a rush as my conduct may have implied, for immediately, on the other side of the storm, I opted to stop for fuel and a bite, turns out the fuel would have to wait on account that the giant canopy that sheltered the fuel lanes were now somewhere in the forest further on.

Off again for the next leg of the trip, a little further west to the semi-arid plains of Oklahoma so to finally get these monkeys off my back, but shouldn't I call them cats as their ballast proved, keepin' all eighteen paws firmly founded throughout the veil of nature's long, mysterious trips. A veil incidentally that must remain otherwise all things would he proved, rendering faith as common knowledge and our gracious God's relationship with us as cheap, which of course it is none of.

TALL WALLS OF TYRANNY

A woman escapes East Germany sometime after the Second World War. perhaps you've seen the old news reels. She does not wish to leave the homeland of her youth, but only it's all-encompassing oppression and its mandated aggression, its new border now a cold prison denying affection, those self-imposed walls and razor-wire taxing patriotism broke.

Longing for liberty, the love of life she following some men you could feel the fright, running down the hill with all of her might! Like hunted birds fleeing the fowler's grasp, the men already through stretch a wider gap in the razor wire: opening for her safer pass, but in a panicky dash, she gets caught on the sharps, her thrust continuing through cuts her violently.

How very sad. But there is no time for sad; Joseph Stalin the Terrible, the butcher of tens of millions of souls has his horde on the prowl. You might suppose a woman being more genteel and delicate would cry or give up, but no, like a broken deer having been struck by a semi, she scrambles off in a sprint.

How horrific the reality of evils extent. Surely evil would to keep her prisoner or it would to kill her better still, but if not, it will settle to wound her, for evil knows that on the other side of those Tall Walls of Tyranny it can dress itself in more subtler ways, but dressed to kill none-theless, all its limited days. The wise will understand that the war is always on, that those who live another day must struggle with evil in yet another way, only do we rightfully pray that evil not be made up in our likeness this or any day for being under evil's sway is "eternally" worse than being it's victim!

Ray Amato
December 2007
Bayside State Prison

IT IS IN GIVING THAT WE RECEIVE

A Christmas Story

A devout clergyman visits a hospital during the Christmas season to bring some cheer and the "Good News" message. Perhaps, he thought, if he found any receptive, he might tell them of the hope that was born in Bethlehem so many years ago. As you will see, the saying "It is in giving that we receive" was perhaps never more clearly realized. His first visit was to an elderly woman who was terminal, so a nurse had told him. Upon his entrance, her energy soared as she invited him to "sit and chat a bit."

"Hello, young man, my name is May," she said, instantly taking command of the room.

"Well, May, you know it snowed last night," he said, "and if it remains cold these next few days, we will have a White Christmas."

She smiled with a reminiscent look, saying, "I remember many white Christmases. Once when Bill and I were still just dating he took me to New York City, we had a grand day shopping, then we took a horse and carriage ride through Central Park. I remember it like it was yesterday, it was evening, dark, you know, under a full moon in a crystal clear sky full of stars. It was quite wonderful and very romantic—oh yes, my Billy was a prince. And as if that wasn't glorious enough, clouds rolled in, then snow began to fall, just enough to coat the ground, it was just beautiful, you know, with those old gas street lamps all along the way and such, I don't like to brag you know…"

"Of course not, May," he said.

"Well, in any event," she continued without a hitch, "that was the night my Bill asked me to marry him."

"Well, what did you say, May?" he asked.

"Oh, heavens, young man, you know what I said." Then she blushed with a smile.

"Did you and Bill have children, May?"

"Yes," she said, "we had a son, Thomas Paul, he brought me those flowers just yesterday and he's coming with his whole family this evening."

"That's nice, May," he said.

"Yes," she replied, "anyway the doctors said we could never have children, but I had faith in God that we would, that's when our little Tommy boy was born. Oh heavens, that reminds me of a story. Can you stay a few more minutes?"

Not waiting for an answer, she said, "You're a nice young man…. Well," she began, "Bill always loved Jesus for as long as he could remember, he told me so, and don't you know my son and his family are the same way. It's wonderful, I'm so blessed. God had only been a passing thought to me you know, until I met Bill, that is. Well, as it turned out, God answered our prayers for a baby, Tommy was special in many ways. He seemed to understand God's love and forgiveness from when he was just a tot. Oh, he got into more than his share of scrapes growing up, but how does the Bible say: 'Forgive us our sins as we forgive others.' Anyway I always trusted that God would see him through. Tommy was a wonderful little boy. When he was just six years old, he asked for a 'shiny red wagon' for Christmas. As I prayed with him at night, Tommy would ask Jesus to remind Santa about that wagon and he promised 'Jesus,' that he would give Him the first ride in it. Now our church, which was just down the street from our home, would every Christmas put up the most beautiful Nativity scene. Well, Tommy got his wagon that Christmas morning then promptly suited up in his leggings, coat, hat, and mittens, of course so to take his wagon for a ride. Those were the days when children all played outside safely, you remember don't you, young man?"

Why bother? he thought and instead simply nodded in the affirmative.

She continued, "I looked to check on him through the kitchen window and what do I see but Tommy pulling his wagon down the sidewalk with the baby Jesus in tow, the baby from the nativity scene, you know."

"Yes, how cute," he thought.

"'Thomas Paul, what are you doing?' I yelled out. 'Don't you remember, Mommy?' he said. 'I promised Jesus the first ride.' 'Oh yes, son, now I remember,' and I didn't know what else to say except, 'Now don't forget to bring Him back.' 'I will, Mother,' he said, as serious and matter-of-factly as could be. Tommy was a good boy. You know,

Pastor, I never really worried about his safety after that day, I knew that Jesus would always keep his angels close and it was a good thing too!"

"What about Bill, May?"

"Oh, Bill was delighted with the boy, that's what he would say when he came home from work. He would say, 'Where's the boy, May?' They would play games and go fishing, Bill taught Tommy to throw and catch and hit golf balls, you know. When Bill got sick, Tommy was just twelve years old. Every day before visiting in this very same hospital, Tommy would go to the chapel and pray to Jesus. I knew Bill was ready to go home, to heaven, you know, but still I went to the chapel for Tommy's sake or so I thought. Tommy would ask Jesus to let his dad stay, but that he would understand. When Bill finally passed, Tommy said, 'Come, Mother, let's go to the chapel.' I felt so sorry for my son, losing his father so young, I just went with him. Tommy's prayer was characteristically simple as always, 'Thank you, Jesus,' he said, 'for taking my dad to your beautiful heaven where he can be happy and strong again until we see him again.' 'You're such a fine and brave boy, Tommy,' I told him. 'I'm sad too, Mother,' Tommy said to me, 'but doesn't a seed have to die so that it may live again? Don't you remember the gospel, Mother? We will see Father again.' 'Oh yes, son, now I do remember I told him, thank you."

"He's right," thought the pastor. "We cling to life as a caterpillar all the while resisting the metamorphosis of the butterfly."

"You know, young man," she went on. "Tommy has given me a lovely daughter-in-law, her name is Rachel and together they have given me three grandchildren. The older two are beautiful identical twin girls. They are sixteen years old and their names are Faith and Charity. I just adore them. My grandson is the baby. His name is William after his grandfather. Little Billy will be six this spring, so I bought him a shiny red wagon for Christmas."

"Well, May," said the Reverend, "I hope you feel better so you can go home soon."

"Oh well, thank you, young man, but Tommy's picking me up tomorrow morning, so I'll be home for Christmas, Lord willing. Then I'll be ready to go home to my Billy and all the rest of our family and friends and Jesus. I won't be sick or old when I get to my true home, you know."

"Yes," he said, "I think I do, now more than ever before." As he turned to leave, saying goodbye, May said, "Merry Christmas, Pastor, I can tell that you are a man of true faith, so don't worry, everything will turn out just wonderfully."

"Thanks for the story, May," he said as he left. "You really cheered me up." *Imagine that*, he thought to himself.

Finally, she said, "I'll see you in the Kingdom by and by, you know," then she smiled…

Seven hundred years before the birth of Christ, the prophet Isaiah foretold of the first Christmas, of the long awaited Messiah. The prophecy was fulfilled in the year one and documented in the new Testament and by the testimony of the Church.

"For a child will be born to us, a
son will be given to us;
And the government will rest on
His shoulders;
And His name will be called
Wonderful Counselor,
Mighty God,
Eternal Father, Prince of Peace.
There will be no end to the increase of His government or
of peace,
On the throne of David and over
his kingdom,
To establish it and to uphold it with
justice and righteousness
From then on and forevermore.
The zeal of the Lord of hosts will
accomplish this.
(Isaiah 9:6–7)

And it gets better, for even beyond Christmas comes
Easter, the day upon which our salvation was accomplished,
and since that day, death no longer has mastery over those
who believe and align themselves with the Prince of Peace,
amen.

COLORS
Sublimely On Sailcloth

An artist imitate "The Artist," an *original copy* of His flora and fauna creation.

It's a pristine autumn afternoon in the rural mountains of New England, the day is warm to comfort, the air dry and clear making all the colors of its foliage and surroundings the brighter. High in the noon sky, the sun is a dazzling yellow-gold accompanied by a scattering of cotton white clouds back dropped by a deep azure blue sky. The blue appears all the more brilliant viewed through the deep green of some giant Tamarack Pines. The breeze is slight and fresh perfumed by the multicolored foliage, wild flowers, and rich black soil of seasons past. In the shallows of the crystal clear lake sunfish scurry tending their sandy nests. A pair of turtles instinctively warm themselves upon some protruding rocks as the evening cool settles upon their valley lake habitat. High up in a white birch by the lake's sole tributary brook a golden finch sings out, "God is good," "all the time," retorts a Robin red breast whose tunes are true and clear, no wonder they say "song beds bring good cheer." Hummingbirds hover among the flowering bushes as a flock of sparrows dart through the thickly populated timbers with speed and agility, but lo and behold, high above the canopy soars the graceful hawk, gliding lighter than air he does not flap, nay, nor flutter a wing, taking time for colors to dry our painter rests from his creating; too, this time affords an interlude for fine-tuning his awareness of details.

As evening approaches, the lengthening shadows of trees and thickets coax some crickets to chirp, they are easily heard, but rarely seen where they take cover under rocks and leaves, in the ford toward the near end of the lake bull flogs find a stealthy placement in amongst tall green grass and reeds of cattails. A thick growth of lily pads with pink flower blooms provide pedestals for these amphibious hunters while busy insects travel the pleasant ways unaware.

The forest is dotted like a Van Gogh painting with shades of burgundy, orange, red, yellow, green, and gold among a myriad of various trees and plants all around, nearby, and upon the distant hills. No doubt the beauty is a deliberate celebration of life, another year's growth all to the glory of "The Artist." Not far yonder an antiquated log cabin of ancient colonial setters gives explanation for the various fruit trees nearby; there are apples for the whitetail deer, blackberries for the bluejays, and stark red cardinals, the blueberry bushes are the claim of the black bears, while the walnut trees delight a colony of gray squirrels who frolic festively in their gathering fields, where God so graciously provides food and shelter as they cheerfully chatter, "all upon our behalf."

In the distance, the faint sound of honking is heard; this clarion call can only mean that Canadian geese are on wing. The call grows louder, clearer as the flock nears out of the western sky with its setting sun whose bright gold has cooled to an orange-red. So close now one can hear the flapping of their powerful wings. As they approach flying into the teeth of a stiff breeze the eye is drawn to the sky above a group of weeping willow trees whose sway decorates the lake shore like great draperies of greenish-gold. Here they come in that typical V formation, a dozen or more birds slowly glide down in what seems like slow-motion cinema, the head wind gently dropping them like so many seaplanes. By comparison, their graceful gliding has digressed to a slow and awkward paddling, not as much to boast about not as glorious a display; nevertheless, the cool water seems to delight them, thirsty and wearied by their journey their assiduous chatter gives away their obvious contentment, for their thrill and glory is in flight, but this placid lake in season is their mother, these hills and fertile fields their home.

A family of deer move through the forest not far off, with the apple harvest over they continue on toward the lush green meadows further on, a powerful buck proudly antlered leads a pair of slender and graceful does, each with her nursing fawn. These passive creatures travel stealthily, almost silent with colors to hide. A great white owl swoops from a high perch, setting off for her nightly hunting grounds, the bats also file out of the crags and clefts to do their duty, thinning the wily and persistent insect population. These nocturnal creatures tell our painter that it's high time to retreat from the forest before dusk yields to dark. Look that other great light that reins at night is coming up full and bright ushering safe passage. Upon leaving, he cannot help but envision other works yet to be painted "sublimely on sailcloth," other original copies of "The Artist's Creation," more "Colors" of this enchanted valley perhaps of springs gentle pastels or of winters hard browns and grays on white in a field of blue.

The painter's brush is really a pen, his palette a legal pad. From within a prison cell, the landscape is in a God-given imagination and a treasure trove of visions and memories, scenes from country roads and highways, of mountains and valleys, of farms and fields and of cities, but mostly for this work, it is from his former home, the circa-1850 Hyson house in Jackson, NJ, with its lovely acre of trees and flowers and critters and from those delightful adventures at Turkey Swamp Park with sweet Robin Red Head and our dogs, Cassy and Handsome Henry, where the forest and fields are natural, where the wild turkeys and deer roam free, and where the Canadian geese gracefully land the lakes and ponds at sunset

Dedicated to Scarlet Rose, my first
grandchild born October 27, 2014.

A DREAM IN REALITY

I had a dream. The following first few pages are the dream as best one can communicate the vagueness of a dream. The balance is my attempt to convey my gut feeling of its purpose and meaning, which if I am not mistaken is the glory God is due for the creation of all things out of no things. So much life everywhere on Earth, occurring in an orderly universe of awesome symmetric beauty. The dream came to me in lock up. Very early in the morning, I arose before the sun to start writing. I felt little option but to write, not because I knew what I was going to write, but only due to the profoundness of such mystery and the strong feelings and energy that filled that confined space.

In the beginning of this dream, I existed in a void, like the void that must have been reality before the universe was created. No Earth or atmospheric heaven (the first heaven). No outer space (the second heaven), nor was it God's most beautiful third Heaven, which we call Heaven or God's Kingdom; read the apostle Paul's personal testimony of the third heaven in 2 Corinthians 12:1–6.

In the beginning, I could not perceive where I was, which would seem reasonable since in a true void, there can be no time or place, no energy, no, not even space for all four phenomenon energy, time, space, and matter had to all occur simultaneously for anything to be, says all reputable scientists. In this case, only God can exist because He, being the Creator, must by necessity predate creation, as well God must be eternal in Himself since He is called the eternal uncreated I AM. Anyway, in the beginning I was strictly spirit, a sickeningly sad and frightened spirit for I was without my five senses, with nothing to see or hear, smell, or touch. I was just a poor soul with former life experiences to recall, but as for that brief time, nothing, like a chronic alcoholic or addict who sleeps but no longer dreams. I somehow simply existed without reason or so it seemed.

I could not see God for He is invisible, but I was beginning to feel His presence as He carried me in His arms across nothing. He began to speak to me audibly, explaining many things in creation, especially about earth and its people some complimentary some not so much. God is most gracious to me, I thought as I was beginning to experience my own existence and that of the creation. I was convincingly sure of the vast differences between creation and Creator. Creation is to be experienced and enjoyed, but the Creator is to be forever praised and honored, a thing to which I have many times failed miserable.

Before experiencing the creation, there was no happiness, no meaning, but only emptiness within and without, no questions, no answer. This terrible emptiness was thankfully short-lived as light appeared, and as I sensed being. Simultaneous to light's appearance, energy soared everywhere and time was born as space had become occupied. Immediately we began to travel, carried in His arms like

Tiny Tim, he took me across the universe. I saw incredible scenes, first billions upon billions of great lights, countless stars in an infinite expanse and the rest as follows.

I have since become convinced that in His presence which by faith we always are I shall never be ultimately afraid since God is all-loving, all-powerful, all-knowing, and everywhere present. He loves everyone and those of us who acknowledge His supremacy will live eternally in His protective embrace. Not just a length of time, mind you but a quality of life, peace, and joy without measure. As the Apostle has said, "Eye hath not seen not ear heard, neither have entered into the heart of man, the things which God hath prepared for them that love Him" (1 Cor. 2:9).

How wonderful, but how and why? Many things written in My Holy Word are understandable, says God, especially your relationship with my Son, your Savior, but many more are mysteries for the time, some things are vague by design affording faith its opportunity while others will remain mysteries in this life, the latter I though should be God's prerogative. He said your faith will be measured in scales of love and deeds since words at times come so cheap. Good deeds he said will be the product of true faith as I produce them through you. I have given all of you life and called all to faith, so chose faith as you pursue life and LIVE!

(I must interrupt this narrative to say...)

If this all sounds a bit extravagant, I ask, how much more extravagant is a self-creating universe full of complex life and countless system and cycles all working in unison without a designer creator. If I met your average smart man or woman or evolutionary scientist and told him, "I found this perfectly rectangular brick with the initials S & F brick company stamped into it, in a clay field and that it was formed by happenstance, I mean by random accident, he would surely tell me I was mistaken if he were a polite man or he would call me a lunatic if he were frankly being more frank and rightfully so. But with his next breath, he might say if he were a proponent of evolution that all complex life on Earth developed by accident as well all the movements of the heavenly bodies, which move like a prima ballerina and count time with greater accuracy then the finest Swiss watch, etc., and so on... So now let's be honest by saying neither creation nor evolution nor even God for that matter are provable items. According to the scientific method, one must in this case observe and record the creation or reproduce it by experiment both of which are obviously impossible. Such honesty gains us credibility; on the other hand proponents of evolution claim that the evolution of the universe and all therein is a fact. So now we have proved one thing and it is this; if one says evolution is a proven fact, he is a liar, so too is the one who claims that God is a "scientific" fact.

Again God spoke, faith is not based on evidence or it would not be called faith; however, I am about to show you my universe full of evidence, behold my laboratory.

To me, this all seems quite scary since more revelation means more accountability to holy living, which up until now I confess I have not done well, yet I write making me even more accountable!

God carrying me traveled across space. I could not measure time or distance since perspective was lost with nothing in which to compare or contrast, but that was about to change.

As the universe came into view, I wondered about all this mind-boggling design. Evidence, indeed, I thought as I saw God's deeds everywhere, billions of galaxies each containing billions of stars of various colors and kinds, all in motion with the grace of—well, of a universe, but what is my reason and purpose? The answer to this question I now understand is the quest and thrust of life. Then for my entertainment God said, "A person walking about on a moving train is moving in five different directions at the same time."

"How so?" I asked.

To which He said, "You have a walking person on a moving train on a revolving planet at a thousand MPH, which orbits the sun at many thousands of MPH, which is part of a galaxy traveling trans universe, that my son is moving in five directions, provided an earthquake doesn't occur, adding a sixth direction." Wow, amusing indeed.

Having spanned many light years in only moments it seemed, I began to focus on one star in particular. "Father, how far is a light-year?" I asked.

"A light-year, my son, is the distance that light travels in one year," He told me. "I was still confused," He continued, light travels at approximately 186,000 miles per second, understanding that I was still confused He said, to put it in perspective, the earth is twenty-four thousand miles around at the equator. Light can circle the globe more than seven times per second, and if one traveled at that speed for one year, he would travel one light-year. I did the calculation and came up with about 6 trillion miles in a year, but that is very hard to understand, Lord, how can I understand even just one trillion?

"Well," He said, "if one spent 1 million dollars a day every day since the birth of my son Jesus, he would not have come close to spending even one trillion dollars by now in 2020." Wow, and the farthest galaxy known to man to date is 13 billion light years away and the nearest star beyond our own sun is four light-years distant. Father, according to the Bible's creation story the universe is relatively young, not the 13 billion years it would take for light to reach earth from that distant galaxy so that we could see it. Is the Bible to be taken literally at every word? Did you create the universe with all stars immediately visible and with all forests tall? He smiled at me then said, "You should understand, it is mine to conceal many matters and the glory of men to find them out and mankind is well on this path."

"What if one could travel faster than light, Father?"

"We are just now doing that very thing," He said, and for that reason, you are not aging at all, in fact you have become slightly younger. It is written that "God is light," and that I am eternal and can transcend time in both directions? He continued some Bible students are wrongly afraid to compare the Bible and science but this is wrong, science means knowledge and I am knowledge, true science has never nor will ever contradict my revelation to mankind i.e. the Bible. On the other hand pseudoscience or false science has many times claimed to raise doubts of my Word, like that laughable evolution fairy tale, don't run from their certificates and titles, do your own work, debate them, be a herald of the truth to babes.

Having traveled so many light-years in only moments, I began to be focused on one star in particular. God said, "They call this star the sun," then He showed me the planets. I took notice of the one called Saturn. Saturn has billions of rocks and boulders that orbit her at her equator. They appear at a distance as multicolored rings or belts suspended around it in space like giant hula hoops. I asked, "Why are those rings there?"

"To show man that I AM, and for your viewing pleasure and because I like them."

"Are there other reasons, Father?"

"Yes, there are," He said and nothing beyond that. Again he spoke, "Look at Jupiter the giant and her many moons sixty one in all. I wondered why Jupiter has moons or satellites, then I caught on, same as Saturn's rings, because He likes them and for our pleasure and for mystery and for many more reason some known by now others not yet. These things are good and so are we because God made us all. I am coming to understand that we were not created to be alone, that we must always strive to know God and live in harmony with our follow man but who would not want to do that?

Our star called sun is yellow in color and small to medium in size and heat compared to other stars. What is that beautiful planet there called, the third one from the sun, I explained as though he needed me to explain. I did not stop for an answer my God-given mind reeling. It was blue and white with green, brown, pink, red, orange, and more. The blue was like a mirror onto space with swirls of white like a giant bowling ball or magnificent marble. Like most of the other planets it had a moon or satellite, but just one. It is big by comparison to its mother planet—about one-third the size. "On this planet you will live," said God, "it is called Earth." Then I asked, what determines the size of Earth's moon.

"It is," God replied, "the very size it needs to be so not to cause floods on earth but still cause tidal movements, the ebb and flow of the oceans. Among other things the tides oxygenate the oceans and clean the bays. Without the moons gravitational pull on Earth's oceans, which is that which causes tides sea life would die and so would land animals due to stagnation and subsequent disease. I have created vast amounts of fish, sea mammals and plant life, millions upon millions of varieties. They are and endless source of food for man and wild animals if care is taken, you will do well to be good stewards of the oceans, bays and rivers. Remember, faith and good deeds work together. In addition, the moon marks time these segments are appropriately called months. The moon is a mild nightlight, making sleep sweet and night travel safe."

"Are there other reasons, Father?"

"Yes," he said, "many others."

"And you like it too, don't you?"

"Yes, I like it too."

"Because it's good, right?"

"Yes, it is good."

God continued, "Do you see that flag, some time ago in the year 1969 AD,[41] a group of your brothers flew in a craft of their own design from Earth to the moon and placed that flag there—the flag of the USA. God seemed proud of them, but it did not seem so great to me at that time, since I was in the presence of the Almighty and had just traveled across a vast universe, but later, I understood. I wondered about this Lord Jesus. He must be very special if the whole world counts time according to His earthly birth, God's Son, begotten not made, oh my! How small am I.

We had come very close to the sun relatively speaking since we first entered this system of planets. What I asked is this system and how is it held intact? "They call it the solar system," God replied.

"The planets orbit the sun in elliptical circuits dragging their satellites in tow by the universal laws of centrifugal force and gravity. You brother Issac Newton discovered these and many other scientific laws in addition to being a prolific inventor, but note, Isaac wrote more on theology that is the Bible and faith than he did on science, and there are many others like him, so much for the idea that smart people don't have faith."

"Anyway," God continued, "especially strong is the gravity that the sun exerts because it is so large, then come planets, moons, etc. according to their size. The sun, however, being more than one million times larger than the earth is massive enough to rule the course of all her planets. For centuries until Copernicus, Newton, Galileo, and oth-

---

41 The year of our Lord.

ers made their discoveries people thought the earth was at the center of the system. It has been interesting to observe mankind's progress in all the sciences.

"Gravity," God continued, "is that which keeps the planets ruled to their orbital limits around the sun. This is especially important to earth's living organisms. You see I have placed earth 93 million miles from the sun, precisely the distance needed in order to control living temperatures for all inhabitants of the various regions. Incidentally, when you look at the sun from earth you are seeing history, I mean the past, since the earth is approximately eight light minutes from the sun, you are seeing the sun as it was eight minutes ago.

For planets, a complete orbit around the sun equals one planet year, which varies due to the different travel distances and planet speed; in Earth's case the time lapse is of course 365 Earth days. A day is counted every time the Earth completes one full revolution on its axis. The axis is affected by the opposite magnetic forces of the north and south poles as well as according to the weights and balances I have built in by mountains, hills, oceans, polar caps, etc., much like the weights a mechanic places on the rim of a tire so that it turns true without wobbling. This revolution creates night and day through a twenty-four-hour period as the sun though in motion is in relation to earth as though standing still."

"Father, how do the heavenly bodies create our seven-day week?"

He responded, "The seven-day week is not in response to the movements in space but instead in accord with my seven days of creation."

"Father, did you really create the universe in seven actual twenty-four-hour days?"

To this question, God smiled then said, "You can figure that one out yourself, many churches have come up with many different determinations, which have caused more trouble than it is worth, keep seeking but live at peace with those to whom you differ."

"I'm sorry for interrupting, Father, please continue."

With a gentle smile, He went on. "Throughout the year, the Earth tilts on its axis, creating seasons the northern hemisphere, has summer when tilted toward the sun, then gradually tilts back, bringing autumn, winter, then new life again with springs return. Winter in the north means summer in the south, while the equatorial regions have little to no seasonal change its always hot while the extreme north and extreme southern regions vary from cold to frigid."

God continued, "I have placed great jungles and tropical forests in the southern hemispheres. Plant life thrives on carbon dioxide then transform it into oxygen, which promote animal life who transform oxygen back to carbon dioxide, it is a perfect trade off as each benefit the other in this recycling process. The wildlife and plants of these regions are wonderfully colored and diverse, be it the tropical rain forests of South America's Amazon or Africa's great grass savannas, Australia, or the numerous islands of the South Pacific Ocean. There are numerous tribes and nations of peoples with various languages spoken. These are your fellows live at peace as best you can." I wondered why should peace be so hard, who would prefer war?

God continued, "Halfway between the equator and the North Pole are areas of dense vegetation and animal life. The majority of Earth's people have settled in these locations due to its intermediate climate. I'm speaking of Europe and North America. Great forests still stand in North America two great mountain ranges, the Appalachians in the east and the towering Rockies in the west, whose trees are good for building. In the central parts are endless flat land with rich soil for farming, also great wild flowered prairies of grassland where grazing animals find endless food and water and easy living. The wild mustangs raced there and the buffalo also roamed literally by the tens of millions on the prairies of the high plateaus and plains of North America in both the USA and southern Canada, but some of your forefathers killed nearly all of them in a couple of decades in the mid- to late-1800s in order to starve out the indigenous peoples—the great Indian nations of the Americas." I could not see God's tears and disappointment but I, no doubt, felt it. We silently and solemnly moved on.

"The extreme north and south have severely colder weather due to their extreme locations," God explained. This is because the sunlight comes to those areas from very shallow angles, the shallow angle means light must cross hundreds of miles of dense atmosphere, quit the opposite of the equatorial regions where the angle is much more directly above in which case the sunlight crosses only ten or fifteen miles of dense air. Put another way, it is why the morning and evening parts of day are cooler. So for this reason, the Arctic areas are largely white with snow and ice; in addition the white reflects the light back to space, instead of collecting or absorbing what little heat that comes in."

As we came very close to Earth, I noticed that the white was not on the ground only but above it as well like floating cotton balls—beautiful. The blue ocean was moving, rising up then falling as though it were breathing. Certainly this planet is unique to anything seeable in all of space. Then God spoke again, "The blue is called oceans, lakes, rivers etc., they teem with life, it is an endless source of food for man and beast if care is taken. The waters like the forests leach oxygen into the atmosphere. In a way, the oceans are breathing; however, the water is not really blue. It is as clear as crystal but appears blue as the sky is reflected or gray when clouds are reflected, but neither is the sky really blue; it is as black as coal but appears blue as the sunlight reflects off the molecules in the atmosphere. Those white swirls floating above collect the rising vapors then eventually once saturated they let drop the dew, rain, or snow so to irrigate the land."

I thought, how amazing all this design with rhyme and reason from a big bang, I mean from a colossal explosion? That is not my experience with explosions. All I can say is, if an explosion is how God started this universe then it was Him who brought it to order, I am not going to ask Him, I think I know His answer. "Father, I can see the aesthetic beauty of the clouds and that they irrigate the forests, fields, and crops but are there other uses?"

"Yes," He replied, "clouds also give needed shade regulating global temperatures, and evening clouds like a blanket retain the daylight heat. The rains from clouds are also a cooling agent, as well it is the most universal solvent on earth, it can be used to produce energy or to turn mills."

"Are there more reasons, Father?"

"Yes," He said, then again, I felt His smile.

It's time to finally touch down on solid earth. First I saw a white fox hunting rodents in the frozen tundra, polar bears riding on ice sheets just off shore, sea birds, and seals. I saw a herd of orcas, carnivorous mammals also called killer whales, then a right whale 55 feet long, a lone bull who eats only plankton. There were schools of fish uncountable in number rushing to and fro, avoiding hunting seals and birds of prey. It was summer in the North Atlantic, but the temperatures reached only 20° Fahrenheit on a still and sunny afternoon. How humble of God to create such great things with no man to see it save a scattering of indigenous hordes called Eskimos or the Inuit peoples who have adapted to this harsh environment. Reading my thoughts, God said, "The fish, birds, whales, and beasts praise me, look at them frolic in festive celebration in the waves see the seals play or the penguins of the south Arctic slide on their bellies like children on sleds. They love life they cling to it by these behaviors they honor me."

Next, we visited the equator. With total polarity to my former experience, it was scorching, hot under a brilliant sun. On the grassy savannas of Africa, I saw agile gazelles and impalas, wildebeests by the hundreds, twenty-foot tall giraffes, hyenas, crocodiles and more. At a muddy watering hole, there were elephants, earth's largest land mammals, the dangerous rhinos cool themselves there, as a troop of baboons drink with one eye on the tall grass where a hunting lion pack is sheltered from the noon sun. There were birds of exotic colors in the trees while the graceful hawk soars above. There are humans in this arid and dangerous land who have learned to make a living; they speak but I do not understand.

Next we came to North America, more specifically my home nation the USA. The west coast was our port of entry with coastal cliffs and rocky outcrops caused by the continual pounding of Pacific Ocean storms. God showed me the lush Sacramento valley growing vegetables and fruit plentiful enough it seemed to feed the world. In the great northwest timber stands are enormous sequoia trees more commonly called red woods growing in excess of 250 feet tall, 100 feet around and living up to 2,700 years long, the largest living organism on Earth. Climbing the Rocky mountains towering heights, I saw the fearsome grizzly bear hunting salmon fish who have returned to the very stream they were hatched in so to mate, this after roaming the open sea for nearly two years. There were mountain goats on the rocky heights, elk in the pastures, hunting pack wolves, coyotes, wild cat of various kind and a plethora of all kinds of other animals, including our national bird, the bald eagle. In the southwest desert region were all sorts of snakes, spiders, scorpions, many of whom with a poisonous bite or sting. The plant life is unique there, like many kinds of cactuses who can live up to two years without rainfall. This desert region ranges from Nevada, Utah, Southern California, Arizona, New Mexico, and part of Western Texas.

Our next stop is the high plains ranging from 1,800 to 7,000 feet above sea level it covers parts of nine states from Montana through Kansas to the panhandle of Texas. The high plains are to the east of the continental divide. The continental divide is the height from which the rain and melted snow shed either east or west according to gravity. It starts in minor creeks which follow ancient courses to streams then rivers, even our great rivers finally making their way to the bays as brackish water a mix of fresh run off water and salty tidal seawater, ending ultimately in the world's oceans to be evaporated up so to repeat this ancient cycle. These high plains were the stomping grounds of the American buffalo also called bison. Great buffalo herds roamed these plains in the tens of millions.

Conservation attempts in the last decades have saved the buffalo from complete extinction. These five-thousand-pound animals who once stretched from horizon to horizon in endless herds it seemed were nearly wiped off the earth in only a few decades in the mid- to late 1800s by foolish, greedy people in effort to starve out the North America Indians and to promote the growth and unimpeded progress of the transcontinental railroad. The brutality and waste must have been staggering, I thought. In their place now are cattle, corn and wheat fields so immense that the high plains and Midwest plains are now known as the great American bread basket, which as a consolation is a good thing, feeding famished people worldwide.

Next we visited the black hills of the Montana territory the sight of the famed last stand of General George Custer, the last major victory of the Indian resistance. It is known to us as the battle of the Little Big Horn. In 1876, the year of our countries centennial Custer and his six hundred troops engaged Sitting Bulls force of ten thousand men. Custar died along with nearly half of his men that frightful day which only strengthened the resolve of the union army leading to the beginning of the end of the Indian's hope of autonomy. In the Dakota territory, we visited a unique mountain with the busts of four men carved into it. Who are these men Father? He told me their names, titles, and of their faith and deeds. He began, "Those are images of outstanding men. First is George Washington, in his youth, George was a surveyor and a farmer, later he lead the Colonial army to victory over Great Britain, then finally the first president of the fledgling United States of America. He knew me and loved my Holy Word. During the Revolutionary War, in lieu of a chaplain, George would read the scriptures to his troops on Sunday and when men would die in the field he would preside over their memorial service. George spent himself serving me by serving others. Next is Thomas Jefferson who was America's third president. Thomas weighed heavily in America's quest for independence, drafting its famed declaration of independence. Ensuring that our sovereign and autonomous nations documents and currency bore my name IE. In God, we trust.

During his administration, your nation doubled in size as a result of the Louisiana purchase. Third is Abraham Lincoln, critics like to point out that Abe struggled with faith as a young man, but I understood his confusion losing his mother and sister as a young boy. Abraham serves as a good example to those called out of a hotter fire; finally however, his faith was a strong tower. Under his presidency, your nation entered the bloodiest time in its history. The Civil War was a horrible time of unthinkable carnage, more than six hundred thousand killed. Reading the constitution, which states "that all men are created equal" left Lincoln no choice but to stand against slavery, leading to the South's secession which was the direct reason for the war. The war was unpopular in both north and south due to the suffering incurred by both and so was Lincoln unpopular in both north and south; in fact he was for a time the most unpopular president to that day. Funny thing is today, he is thought by most as the greatest president ever. Let this be a lesson of the fickle and emotional judgments of mankind, don't take them to serious son.

Fourth comes Theodore Roosevelt, a rough and tumble man exploring the then mysterious Amazon River as an elderly man but in his youth a boxer, big game hunter, governor of New York, secretary of the Navy, and president of the United States. During the Spanish-American War, which took place in Santiago, Cuba, Teddy volunteered and organized the famed rough riders who were a decisive and pivotal force leading to victory in 1898. In 1903, Theodore led our country in the greatest dig in world history to date, the Panama Canal. It is to this day, a shortcut from the Atlantic Ocean to the Pacific Ocean, saving thousands of miles of sailing distance. In honor of me and in appreciation of my creation, Teddy created national parks all over the nation for man's recreation and as preserves for my wildlife.

As we were leaving Mount Rushmore, the early sunrise shown upon the faces on that mountain a red blush as though the four men heard their Lord's praise. I became excited to join such a good people in their pursuit of life, of knowing and serving so great a God. Later, though, I came to understand that that was not always man's first concern nor to be honest has it always been mine. As I consider the good men and women of the past I find this reverence of God a common thing. In fact just in my own life time this has changed noticeably. I think mostly due to our educators (especially higher learning), the arts and the media with their God is dead evolution and other ill religious liberal notions.

Next, we turned due south along a big muddy river called the Mississippi. Alongside it were flat plains of rich soil, farms everywhere in all directions. There are also numerous towns and cities, which use her watery highway for industry and to transport their produce and other goods, from Minneapolis in the north to St. Louis to Memphis to the extreme south at New Orleans the queen of the delta where the river terminates at the Gulf of Mexico.

Now its east-southeast to the sunshine state a peninsula called Florida. Explored and named Florida by Ponce de Leon in 1513. Florida is a Spanish word meaning "Full of Flowers" there are fruit trees in abundance yielding oranges, tangerines, grape fruits, lemons, limes, and more. Also strawberries and winter vegetables for the temporarily dormant northern states and Canada. I almost forgot the vast sugar cane whose fields perfume the Floridian air at harvest time. A popular vacation destination for swimmers, boaters and fisherman Florida boasts thousands of miles of coastline with white sand beaches on both the Atlantic Ocean and Gulf of Mexico. Really a gigantic sandbar whose average above sea level is a mere six feet, save in a few places near Orlando and on the panhandle where her capital city of Tallahassee lay. Florida boasts the widest river in the world. The Everglades that flows south out of Lake Okeechobee is a wildlife refuge containing alligators, uncountable as well as an exhaustive list of tropical birds from flamingos to parakeets and mammals from the rare Florida panther and black bear to the multitudinous deer, muskrat and armadillo. Offshore are an abundance of big game fish: tarpon, sailfish, swordfish, and sharks. Florida's intercoastal waterways are a playground for dolphins, manatees, whales, and other amphibious mammals.

Incidentally, my dream was brief, but in any case, I am not embellishing since as a tractor trailer road driver for more than a decade, I truly saw most of these places and the Lord is always with me—with us. We traveled by now as far south as one can travel in the continental United States at Key West Florida. We now turn back north to the main land at Miami. It is night and Miami is lite up like a jewel with its high hotels, showing off her white foamy surf. Next stop is the Spanish colony of Saint Augustine, North America's first settlement in 1565 with a relativly undisturbed landscape of grassy dunes and palm trees a place one must see to believe. Skipping by the Daytone speedway and crossing the Saint John's River at Jacksonville we next came upon the historic city of Savannah in the Peach State called Georgia. Savannah derives her name from the tall green grasses that seem to come out of the sea itself invading the land like a massive friendly green monster sprinkled with a scattering of the world's most diverse varieties of pines and palms. A little farther north, we visited the outer banks of North Carolina. More specifically a town called Kitty Hawk where the Wright brothers successfully achieved the first powered flight. This first flight traveled only 120 feet for the duration of twelve seconds. Only sixty years after this first successful flight the USA landed their first men on the moon. Lord, now I'm beginning to understand how great an achievement that moon landing really was and the first flight too for that matter.

It was overcast and drizzling as we came upon Norfolk, Virginia. Brave protectors, the intrepid ships of the US Navy seem to be resting in their berths. Gray ships camouflaged in gray water as the somber sky is reflected. God pointed out ships that fought the greatest sea battles ever commenced in all history. Cruisers, aircraft carriers, and destroyers that sailed the Atlantic and South Pacific during World War II. Those brave men and ships saved the world from those anti-Christ dictators who by name were Adolf Hitler of Germany, Benito Mussolini of Italy, and Tojo Hideki of Imperial Japan. Fight, war, destroy, kill—what and why, I wondered. Then God spoke, "I have given man free will so that I could find pleasure in the fact that men and women chose me. If I created people with no choice but to love and obey me how could I find satisfaction in it. If you could implant a computer chip in your sons and daughters so that they would automatically love and obey you without options would you do it? Of course not, it is their choosing to love you that means everything. I as well have given evil just enough rope to hang itself, if it chooses to, but remember you have a Savior who takes away your sins removing them from you as far as the east is from the west and also remember I want very much to receive you all as sons and daughters. As many as will come. Your Heavenly home is not only beautiful and abundant in all good things, but it is also eternal in time and space."

"Will our animals be in heaven also, Father?"

He just smiled and said, "Your utmost happiness will be my concern."

What a sublime place this planet is, I thought. Traveling due west a sunset shown down upon Richmond, Virginia, the once capital of the southern confederacy. The city that had fallen 160 years before is once again a thriving metropolis peacefully seated in the foot hills of the Blueridge mountains. God showed me fields of notorious Civil War battles. The Battle of Bull Run, Chancellorsville, Fredricksburg, Shilo, and the most deadly of all, the Battle of Antedium with over ten thousand casaulties in a twelve-hour battle, but we have left out so many more like Gettysburg with an additional twenty-three thousand casualties in three days; thankfully this was the beginning of the end of this horrible affair. Moving on to the west, we found ourselves in a grand place of farms and wilderness with quaint villages and hamlets sprinkled here and there. Between the Blueridge Range and the mountains of the wild and wonderful state of West Virginia is a place known as the Shenandoah Valley as beautiful as its name. A number of my writings were done in this inspirational place of wildlife, trees, farms and flowered fields.

Northeast we go to Philadelphia the staging place of the Declaration of Independence in 1776 as Washington, Adams, Hancock, Jay, Franklin, and Jefferson among others forged and signed that declaration, fifty-six contributors in all, which according to King George of England were committing a treasonous act, consequently Benjamin Franklin informed these fifty-six men, "We must all hang together or we shall all hang separately." Hence, the coming war against the world power of that day. Nearby Trenton New Jersey is where General Washington and his men crossed the Delaware River on a freezing cold Christmas night taking by surprise the Hessian's (German mercenary soldiers hired by the king). We then looked over other NJ battle sights Princton, Monmouth, Millstone, Bound Brook, Short Hills, and Fort Lee. Newark, NJ, where most of my road trips originated is a great center of commerce and travel, rail heads, ports, and residences. From Philly to Newark as in all big cities I saw oppression, fatherless children, drug addiction, homelessness, and greed living together with privilege and wealth.

I saw men and women young and old failing at life because they were in many cases so carelessly and clumsily lead. Their government, pretending to care as sick people are swept under a rug called prison. On the lighter side, my home state New Jersey is a good place with mountain country to the Northwest the Kittatinny Range is part of the greater Appalachian Range. Here people work and play, hunt, fish, mountain climb, and ski. It is a wonderfully historic place whose first colonies were settled near the ocean and bays and along rivers as shipping was the most convenient form of transport. The earliest settlements occurred in the 1600s more than 150 years before our independence. The village of Old Bridge just a few miles from my home town of Sayreville dates back to 1634.

New York City is perhaps the greatest city in the world with approximately 8 million calling the Big Apple home. It is commerce, it is art of every conceivable kind; it is home and holiday. Manhattan Island appears regal viewed from her harbor where Lady Liberty or the Statue of Liberty stands welcoming arrivals since 1886 when France gifted it to us. The Apples glass sheathed building look other worldly as the rising sun is reflected back from their towering heights. I noticed a void, an ugly hole in the ground. I looked to God who decried, "The Twins are no more along with thousands of your brothers and sisters."

I hate when God is sad, but what could be said, why, I wondered, must these sad things happen? I got no answer; we solemnly moved on. We moved three hundred or so miles northwest to NY's second largest city Buffalo then across the Niagara River to Canada. The Niagara is the shortest major river in the world. Only about thirty miles long, a tremendous volume of water runs through continuously finally dropping 167 feet over the famed and beautiful Niagara Falls as Mr. Gordon Lightfoot sang, "Lake Ontario take in all Lake Erie can send her."

The Lord and I have been all over this country including Canada and the Mexican border. It is fitting then that we end our trip where it all began the near eastern town of Plymouth Massachusetts where in 1620 our early fore-fathers landed at Plymouth Rock. We lovingly call them simply the Pilgrams, which means "people who journey to a sacred place for religious reasons." And that is precisely what they did. Composing and signing the "Mayflower Compact" before disembarking the ship. It was a legal writ of their laws and purpose as they came here for religious freedom and to evangelize the natives of this new land.

So what was this paper about? It was inspired by a dream of God carrying me across space to the Earth. But the dream was vague and brief. What was not vague at all was what I wrote through the illumination that has come to me by a lifetime of God consciousness, His Spirit with me throughout it all be it thick or thin, happy or sad, profitable and righteous living or loss pursuing my own misguided interests.

The paper was a brief and basic review of history, science, geography, and human behavior as we relate to each other and the rest of creation. It shows God's providence and forgiveness, that He cares for the smallest of details. That we must live under free will, enjoying or enduring those results. It explains the relationship God longs to have with us, what He expects from us and what we can expect from Him.

It explains that God is creator of all things in the universe including the crown of creation—mankind. That men are responsible to believe in God according to the amount of revelation which has three categories: (1) the physical universe which apart from him could not exist; (2) conscience, the knowledge of right and wrong which all peoples of all regions on earth are privy to. It is built into all by the Spirit; (3) the Written Word—the Bible. Those not having access or knowledge of it are nor held accountable to it. How do I know this you ask? Because God is just and thoroughly loving. This does not mean men are better to not have the Bible on the contrary, for we are commissioned to carry this Good News to the farthest end of the Earth. Listen to an authority—the great evangelist and Apostle Paul from his letter to the Romans, which he also calls his gospel. Read Roman in its entirety for fuller context, but for convenience, a few verses dealing with man's responsibility whether Gentiles, Barbarian, or Greek generally meaning those outside the faith and without God's Revelation. Or the Jew or Christian who have access to all three Revelations.

> Because what may be known of God is manifest in them, for God has shown it to them. For since the creation of the world His invisible attributes are clearly seen, being understood by the things that are made, even His eternal power and God head, so that they are without excuse. (Rom. 1:19–20)

> For as many as have sinned without law will also perish without law, and as many as have sinned in the law will be judged by the law for not the hearers of the law are just in the sight of God, but the doers of

the law will be justified; for when Gentiles, who do not have the law these, although not having the law, are a law to themselves, who show the work of the law written in their hearts, their consciences also bearing witness and between themselves their thoughts accusing or else excusing them in the day when God will judge the secrets of men by Jesus Christ, according to my gospel. (Rom. 2:12–16)

God is spirit and eternal. He created us also as spiritual beings—also eternal. We are meant for relationship with creation but especially with creator. This is our reason and purpose in life; it is the quest and thrust of life itself. King Solomon explains, "It is God's purpose to conceal a matter and the purpose of kings to find them out." God reveals many things but much mystery remains. Again it is our goal to understand, but our faith weighs heavily in the balance. To know God is not a matter of knowledge only, hardly for sure, but faith expresses itself in love.

In this dream, I saw examples of selfless service. Washington, Lincoln, Jefferson, and so many more who spent themselves in service along with the simple solders who toiled for freedom—for us their posterity. Following the example of our Lord Jesus, God's own begotten Son who gave Himself up for our sake—the forgiveness of sin. The dream explains our duty as stewards, it explains also the death of buffalos and of men and of freedom, which occurs when stewardship is abandoned or deferred.

PSALM 8:1, 3, 6, 7, 8, 9
O Lord, our Lord,
How excellent is your name in
All the earth
Who have set your glory
Above the heavens!
When I consider your
heavens, the work of your
fingers,
The moon and the stars,
which you have ordained,
You have made him (man) to have
dominion over the works of
your hands;
You have put all things under
his feet,
All sheep and oxen—
Even the beasts of the field
The birds of the air,
And the fish of the sea
That pass through the paths of
the sea.
O Lord, our Lord,
How excellent is your name in
All the earth!

My Grandfather
Andrew Amato
A Purple Heart Recipient

My grandfather Andrew (Andy) Amato who I knew well until his passing at age eighty-eight (when I was about thirty-three) was your quintessential old-time gentleman. Born in 1906, a first-generation Italian American, Pop enjoyed the sports of team rowing upon the then clean Passaic River and was a strong wrestler at Barringer High School in Newark, New Jersey. Pop was also an accomplished ballroom dancer; he and Grandmother Emma who we lovingly called Nan won a number of dance contests back in the old days. At my wedding to Donna Jean, Pop was asked to dance by nearly every woman in attendance and I should mention. He didn't seem to mind one bit. Nan and Pop would visit nearly every Sunday after church for dinner; it was most often pasta and Nan's famous garlic roast beef or eggplant parmesan.

Pop loved to learn but as was common in those days he was forced to quit school before graduation so to help his parents to support his seven brothers and one very protected little sister. In spite of the abrupt end to his formal education pop was well informed. My dad explained, "It's because he reads everything he can get his hands on." I'm sorry to say I never tried very hard in school but later in life due in part to his influence I too became a reader and a writer (if I may be so bold). After the Second World War Pop became the manager of a "Prince Range" appliance store on Springfield Ave., Newark, NJ, until he retired in the early 1970s. The Prince Range Company was a popular chain back then and Pop would write all the speeches for his friend Mr. Shultz who was the owner of said stores.

My dad told me the story of how Pop handled a robbery at his store during the infamous Newark riots of the 1960s, which sprang up in various intercity neighborhoods nationwide after the assassination of Dr. Martin Luther King. "Three armed men came into Pops store," he told me, "forcing everyone to lie down on the floor which everyone promptly did except of course old Andy, who quietly said, 'You can take the money but you will not make me lie on the floor like a dog and so the robbers plan was thus amended.'"

My most proud memory, however, of grandfather concerns his "Purple Heart" service to our great country during the Second World War. Pop was drafted at age thirty-five even though he was married to the matriarch of our family faith, Emma Tartaglia Amato, who together already had three young children when he departed for basic training (I think it was Fort Dix in NJ). My dad Raymond George was the baby at seven years old, my two uncles Norman, eight years, and Donald who everyone called Sonny was ten.

Pop was born just after the advent of the telephone, radio, car, and airplane; he grew up in the rough streets of the ironbound section of Newark. It seemed fighting for his beloved country (like most men of that great generation) was never given a second thought. The army considered sending Pop to Officer Candidate School owing to his high score on their written test; however, the urgency and peril of our nation and frankly of the whole world due to the tyranny of that axis of evil prohibited it. Instead they slapped on his shoulders the two strips of a corporal and a small mortar cannon crew, also specializing as gas experts because of the use of it by Germany in World War I. Thanks to God its retaliatory deployment was never forced.

Once when Pop, Dad, and I were watching a documentary with real film clips from the battle of the Bulge, Pop kiddingly said to me in his remarkably deep voice, "Raymond, did you know I was an noncommissioned officer during the war?" Just as I became greatly impressed, Dad burst the bubble, saying, "That means he wasn't an officer." Then we all cracked up, not least Pop. Nevertheless, I will always remember him as an officer and a gentleman.

Immediately after basic training, Pop shipped off for North Africa joining the commencement of our nation's first theater of action, the code name for the assault was "Operation Torch." Grandfather served mostly under the generalship of "Old Blood and Guts" George S. Patton. Their flotilla split into three groups landing on as many beaches of the Moroccan coast converging on the capital of Casa Blanca, taking it and a strategic airfield, which they did in the face of a hot navel bombardment, thence eastward they trod through Algeria, Tunisia, to the shores of those olden Tripoli pirates finally meeting our British Allies who had come west through Egypt. Once North Africa was liberated they crossed the Mediterranean for the invasion of Sicily so to liberate the good Italian people who were forced at the tip of a spear to fight. At some point in this campaign, a number of soldiers including Pop shipped off to England to be readied for an even more daring and ominous task, the invasion of Europe proper. When a narrow window of favorable weather conditions occurred in the notoriously turbulent English Channel the word was "Go!" And go they did dutifully and wide-eyed. It remains to this day the greatest flotila of men and ships in history 156,000 men and equipment on more than 6,000 vessels bound for the Normandy coast of France; they called it D-Day, June 6, 1944. I don't recall which beach grandfather landed, but probably due to his extensive action already in Africa and Italy he was spared being among those most dangerous early waves of men. After securing the beaches they rigorously pushed on toward Paris to liberate our old helpful friends of the American Revolution.

The two great tank commanders of North Africa will meet again; George S. Patton and Germany's infamous field Marshall Erwin Romel AKA that Desert Fox. Fighting primarily alongside Canadian troops they advanced toward Germany at the interior of the continent more specifically the Riendland where the most violent battle did ensue; it was dubbed "the battle of the bulge" where victory came with no little effort and with great carnage on both sides. Also this was the last great battle on European soil as we met our other major ally Russia in the heart of Berlin, the capital had fallen, victory in Europe!

Finally, the German monster was defeated as was Italy earlier; however, the war was still boiling hot in the South Pacific Islands as Japans leaders vowed to fight to the last man.

Grandfather found himself on yet another ship steaming full speed ahead toward Japan so to be numbered among the invaders of her mainland. Such an endeavor, however, promised more casualties then we were willing to endure. Consequently, President Truman with great anguish decided to drop atomic bombs on two Japanese cities, not only ending the war but most definitely saving lives in the long run, it no doubt saved American lives, and don't forget who was the aggressor. Does anyone recall that day of infamy, that cowardly Japanese attack on Pearl Harbor! And that is the end of my apology; nonetheless, we still morn the colossal casualties of the innocent Japanese populous, same as the common Italian and German citizens.

Before closing this wartime story, I wish to reiterate in poetic style a couple of scenes, which Pop described. One of D-Day, the other which took place over England during his brief furlough there. Mind you, there were never any gory details; in fact when I was a very young boy, I asked him if he ever killed anybody, to which I received only a look. It was then that I understood to never ask any soldier that question again.

Airiel Battle over London

From a trench English children watch their
Nobel country men fight in skilled flight,

the gangious bombers under Hitler's imposed night.
Screaming engines of hurricanes and spitfires
out grace the willful kings giant drowning bombers
Look now at the children's faces pride has ban-
    ished fear,
They are childishly brave, for sure the Lord is near.

THE BEACH AT NORMANDY

Go was the command in the face of German
machine guns on the high cliffs of Normandy.
Did you ever wonder just what goes through
A soldiers mind as an enemy bullet cuts his
soul asunder?
Terror the fear of death or perhaps a curious
calm exhaling his last breath
Their immortal spirits eternally stand
their lifeless bodies calmly sleep in sinking sand.

Like us all Nan and Pop experienced many joys in life, like
the above VE Day or like laughter around the kitchen table
or Fourth of July cookouts or weddings and new babies—
scores of them. But on the other hand, they had to endure
their share of grief. They buried their forty-six-year-old boy
Sonny, a former Marine. A few years later, they laid to rest
their grandson, my cousin David who was just nineteen.
Pop was speechless, but Nan broke all our hearts saying as
she walked from David's grave, "I'm going to tell Sonny
that David is here," and so she did. A decade later, we buried my father. More unforgettable words as Pop standing
before Dad's casket cried out, "My baby boy." Dad was a
day shy of sixty years when he left us. A few months later,

Pop died as gracefully as he lived. Nan passed a few years later also in her late eighties, though true to her nature less calmly then Pop, perhaps that's why it is mostly men who are chosen for combat.

Some may think this sad ending a bit much, but I disagree. To me, sorrow is as much to be embraced as joy. For a life without sorrow would betray a life devoid of love and appreciation, which is the state of spiritual death, a most pitiable state of being. Rather, as people of faith in our God of love we have life now and a future hope, "And hope does not disappoint," says the apostle. And as Jesus had said, "Most assuredly, I say to you, unless a grain of wheat falls into the ground and dies, it remains alone, but if it dies, it produces much grain" (John 12:24).

So now we may conclude, according to the testimony of the above-esteemed witnesses that those of us of faith will all be gathered together again in the great bye and bye, to the place where love and sorrow and faith have lead us, but in that hallowed place only love remains, because faith will become fact and sorrow abolished, amen!

> "And God will wipe away every tear from their eyes." (Rev. 21:4a)

Poetry
and
Proverbial
Section

Ray Amato
December 2000
Lakehurst, N.J

IT'S ALL IN HOW
YOU LOOK AT IT

From within high fences wrapped and capped with razor wire, some do write in reflection; others write best in the city, some in the wilderness, yet others from cheap motel rooms. It's all in how you look at it.

I saw a smiling man in a wheelchair, but frustration on the faces of strong men. Mundane work may cause one to wish his life away, while when with his maiden, he would to stay young. It's all in how you look at it.

"I've seen the needle and the damage done," said Mr. Young, "a little part of it in everyone, and every junkie's like a setting sun." I know Neil is right, from my own prior dilemma rescue's cost was prison, no doubt a sovereign decree that brought freedom through bondage, it's all in how you look at it.

"To live is Christ," said the Apostle, "but to die is gain." In a strictly physical sense, however, it is better to be a poor living man than a dead King. It's all in how you look at it.

A rich man dying of thirst in a barren desert would give all his wealth for a cup of water. To the poor addict a million dollars would seem a dream come true, though in truth it would most likely be the means by which he died, it's all in how you look at it.

"Two men were in prison, both looking through bars, one saw only the mud, the other the stars." It's all in how you look at it.

It is a matter of record, that soldiers of both North and South, who had been killing each other before the South surrendered had afterward met in the middle of that Civil War battlefield and embraced and wept. *I insist*, it's all in how you look at it.

Happiness or better contentment needs to be judged with all things weighed, thus is relevance reckoned. After all, if God be for us who can ultimately prevail against us and who can ruin our day, relevance is what makes even death a victory, when seen through eyes of faith. Yep, it's all in how you look at it.

On the lighter side, me and this bird were hangin' out, you know, me on my motel balcony and him on his telephone wire. You know, two spirited beings wondering just what the other was thinking. He eyeballs me and I him, now what's that all about, you ask? I don't know, this one stumps me, but one thing I do know, whether I look through bars or from a cheap motel balcony, or from my own fine home someday, I should always see my life in all relevance and be happy, I mean content with thankfulness. You've all heard about the man who cried he had no shoes until he met the man with no feet; it's all in how you look at it.

Written not far from the infamous "Hindenburg" crash sight from a cheap motel in Lakehurst, New Jersey.

OCJ
Toms River, NJ
8-16-13

THE WISDOM OF MODERATION

Even a fool may be thought wise if he
speaks not,
And a wise man may be thought a fool
if he speaks too much.
Over-weening pride says, I am wise.
False humility says I'm a fool.

But moderation says
I am a man created!
In the image of God!
By God! I am just a man.

LORD POTTER

Men look to the heavens, now with fright,
    now with delight,
Wondering between the grand physical
    and the abstract invisible,
Just how, who, what, where and why am I,
    is there truly a Great Potter on high?
We are vessels of clay drawn from the earth,
    spirits borne along, toward our birth,
Alive before the Potter fully formed us,
    known only by Him before human eyes
    could behold us,
before human souls could conform us.
Not by random chance in a cold billion years
    but by design with incomprehensible reason
      He created us capable of joy and tears.
Pots do tumble and vessels do fall
    hence the endowment of both
      bestowed in us all.
From whence does the violence come
    that doth dash the pottery to pieces?
They are very old
    those who would to covet His beloved,
      His lambs from among the fold.

By and by the pots
    are no worse for ware
As such fractures present opportunity
    the Potters loving repair.
Though brokenness is painful and through it we cry,
    it leads us back to the Great Potter in the sky
He will mend us again and again
    as long as we try,
Serving others and He
    the Great Potter on high.
So return to The Potter as often as you can
    not only when your broken but even as you
    mend.
When hurt turns to anger return to your Maker
    for those who refuse remain angry and alone.
For the angry young man only the Potter can care,
    for all the rest have their own troubles,
and none more can they bear…

"A man who has friends must
    himself be friendly,
But there is a friend who
    sticks closer than a brother."
                  (Proverbs 18:24)
                      NKJV

"Let patience have her perfect work. Statue under the chisel of the sculptor, stand steady to the blows of his mallet. Clay on the wheel, let the fingers of the divine Potter model you at their will. Obey the Father's lightest word: hear the Brother who knows you and died for you." (George Macdonald)

TRUISM

The revenge of the wicked;
and we are all wicked,
Is the death of the judge;
and we are all judges.
A lethal alloy doubly prone to corruption;
we are all wicked judges.
All thanks be to God our Father, no
less for Christ Jesus our Savior,
through whom "mercy triumphs over judgment."

CONCERNING CRITICISM

Think not of what people think of your thinking:
Whenever they are wrong to think it, or
Whenever their thinking is wrong, or
Whenever what their thinking is wrong of them to think, but
Whenever they are thinking rightly of your thinking wrongly
by all means do think again.
Yes, the first man should mind his own business.
The second has mistaken your intentions.
The third is an enemy trying to do you harm.
But the fourth: is a friend

I think we often get these thoughts inverted, that is, we often worry about what people think, so we explain ourselves to fools and enemies, but when a friend ventures that hapless and unprofitable business of informing us that we are wrong; when we are wrong, we often pridefully recoil in anger, refusing to hear them. Someone had well said, "Familiarity breeds contempt." AND King Salomon explains, "The blows of a friend can be trusted, but one's enemies multiplies kisses." It seems whether one's enemy criticizes or complements he is the enemy and the opposite can be true of one's friends. But let's not forget we victims also play the fool at times and relative comparisons do not excuse.

Now think rightly of how often we err in our thinking, patiently putting up with those who judge our intentions wrongly or with those who are wrong to judge our intentions, yet to the ones who are right in showing us our wrongs we revile in protest, making excuses and killing love as we attempt to defend the indefensible. We often become aggressive toward our friends; angry and cross, we cut off our nose to spite our face, while in truth the anger visits upon our own spirits horridly and the spite casts its dark shadow over our own souls, but also over the souls of our friends who are after all only mere men. We are right to think of this type of thinking as thinking wrongly.

But of course, all the above is easier said than done.

Ray Amato
Jan. 2016
So. Amboy, NJ

Foxhole Prayers are Most Fervent

Question: Why does God allow hard and
painful things to happen to us?

Well, the short answer is, all sunshine makes a desert, for everyone knows that the brilliance of sunshine loses its charm in a barren desert. I mean, a diet of only easy and pleasant things would make of us all ungrateful, wayward assuming prigs. But now, for one slightly longer answer among the myriad, which might be offered:

Throughout the course of life's events, most of us have frequented deaths violent doorstep enough times to know that such occasions occur like clairvoyant still pictures that do quite reveal God's firm position as real. They do not enlighten as the morning star, that is, gradually at dawn, but rather they come unannounced in and instantaneous flash, like a car crash or a fall or a gunshot. I mean, if we cannot find God in the sunshine of life, then such violent events should be considered merciful, even gracious. Because seriously folks, must a man light a candle to see the sun. In any event, God does sometimes enlighten us in such a fashion.

There does, however, seem to be an ever-present danger, and it is this, the sun that makes life possible will if stubbornly glared at for too long render one blind, but just how long that is only God knows. This absent-minded, even disrespectful complacency is a dangerous crap shoot in the light of eternity.

"Show me a sign, God," I foolishly thought as I look to the sky. How contemptuously flippant could I be? As though the creator of the universe we're some kind of trickster, or clown, or like some kind of trite magician for hire. Again with the petition: show me a sign as I looked to the sky more intently for a miraculous or anomalous image perhaps. Trying so hard to see, I failed to see the plain and continuous miracle always before me. Just then as a drifting cloud passed beyond the sun it's brilliant light shown clearly in my heart and mind; eureka, I thought, God has moved the cloud with His breath and the sun has allowed me to see.

Now finally I thought, that is true enlightenment, but I am rarely so enlightened, rather on my own, I am less like the sun and more like that shroud of a cloud in two ways— no, better make it three:

1) The Lord has made us both.
2) Both are a sign of His sovereign creative genius, toward anyone looking for a sign.
3) And both block the light of the sun.

Might not these violent clairvoyant flashes be deliberately permitted by God so to revive by shock treatment, the thoughtless, wayward daydreamers that we do all seem at times? I know one thing for sure, I mean, by repeated experience and that is that no prayers are ever so fervent as those uttered in foxholes.

In any and all events, however, we of faith can be eternally thankful that we have an advocate in God's beloved Son—Jesus the Brilliant One, our Good Shepherd who is patient, gracious and merciful, so merciful a shepherd that He's willing to carry us after He makes us lame, which he does for our training. This may seem odd to some, but it is called God's Word to us and it is very Good News for such needy and absent-minded souls as we can all at times be.

Again I say, perhaps this is one explanation of why God allows hard and painful things to happen to us. For they are at bottom merciful drawing us back (as the Apostle so beautifully stated it), "to our first love," drawing us back, that is, to the sunshine of his presence. On the other hand, it justifies God's judgment toward those who continually resist His calling.

In closing, I will quote, Jesus himself as Mark records Him in his Gospel:

"For what will it profit a man if he gains the whole world, and loses his own soul?" (Mark 8:36, NKJV)

Ray Amato
Ocean Co. Jail
October, 2013

FREED BY THE WHITE DOVE

NIGHTFALL

Aurora Borealis splashed on a star-spangled sky
   at night
      frozen halo 'round a harvest moon
         wolves howl in deft delight
In a valley meadow does graze a graceful doe
   upon the yonder mountains black bears pre-
   pare in woe
For the nights are growing cooler now
   winters not far off
See the summer swans head south
   lo up, up aloft
But behold the approaching Canadian geese
   all a fluttering brakes
Coming in over the willows gently down
   skidding they land these pristine lakes

DAYBREAK

The bright and morning star is paled to pink
by the steamy fogs ascent

But soon autumns reds, greens, and golds
make plain their full intent
As the high noon sun
has far less canopy to rend

EVENING

As Twilight falls all colors fade
on this undefiled wonderland
Stars now sing as birds give way
all 'round North Umber-land
Nova Scotia is a place
I've always longed to see
But two long years in a cold dark cage
I truly be
Rather in spirit I do certainly will
and so now I say
Truly in North Umber-land am I
this very fine day
I think tomorrow I'll sail the sound
and visit Thunder Bay
    or get all dressed down in gray
        in attempt to proper pay
           my respects at Normandy
Or perhaps I'll travel south southeast to African
    Timbuktu
or back out west to that Michigan town at Kalamazoo
Or maybe further west still to Oshkosh by Gosh
so to get my fill
For the spirit cannot be chained nor contained

saved by our own free will
May God forbid it do never pray
for according to free will we must choose our own
     way
But those free by the White Dove will most often
     be gay
even in a cold dark cage as I am today

OCJ
Toms River, NJ
8-16-13

CREATIVITY IS HEREDITY

We must create at whatever level.
It is energy itself, it makes one alive to
create and to appreciate creation. For
we have been created in the likeness
and image of—you guessed it,
The Creator!

FORGIVENESS TRUMPS SIN

"Oh no," said Christian to Grace and Charity,
　　"those nimble
Quick Witted have gone and called Deep Waters
　　dumb"!
"Oh no, indeed, Christian," replied the deep ones,
　　"but is not their
deafness due to the loudness of their shallow
　　rapidity?"

And much like this goes the usual course of human psychology, as the deaf and the dumb call each other blind. Truly lack of humility shrouds in darkness not only the quick of wit and the stoic sophisticate, but all humanity. For as it is written; all are born in sin, and the common denominator beneath all sin is self-pride and the common denominator beneath our being forgiven is our generosity in forgiving others.

"For if you forgive others for their transgressions, your heavenly Father will also forgive you." (Matthew 6:14)

"For judgment will be merciless to one who has shown no mercy; mercy triumphs over judgment. (James 2:13)

"Let love be without hypocrisy. Abhor what is evil; cling to what is good. Be devoted to one another in brotherly love; give preference to one another in honor..." (Romans 12:9–10)

"Above all, keep fervent in your love for one another, because love covers a multitude of sins." (1 Peter 4:8, NKJV)

AMEN?

PROVIDENCE

Might we mistake God's gifts to us
as common material haphazardly found
or worse yet earned?
Perhaps we might.
For even the religious elite of the high Sanhedrin
mistook for a common man,
even for a heretic,
our Lord Jesus.
The very Christ of God
and all this in the midst
of His earthly capital,
Jerusalem City.
Receiving God's gifts without thanksgiving
is to eat and drink judgment,
yea, even to live under its roof.
This must continue for as long as we persist,
for man's greatest gain is found
in God's good pleasure.
And God's good pleasure is giving gifts to His children.
An arrangement simply accepted,
if not it can be learned,
but never forced
and certainly never earned.

TRIALS, PERSEVERANCE, THANKSGIVING

If there were not mixed with blessings also; worry, anger, sorrow, cold, hot, hunger, sickness, etc., than certainly, there could be no faith in all the earth, no contentment thus little blessings for hopelessly ungrateful people.

Without suffering, wants, needs and longings there would be no true happiness, no contentment, no thankfulness and no adoration toward our providential God and Savior, I mean, there would be no salvation consequently, it would seem. If true, this would be all in all most tragic and prone to a far more thorough and everlasting suffering, eternal separation from God, I mean.

Does anyone see God's wisdom and method here? Neediness, from our daily bread to our salvation are that which drive us to our knees; the low place where hope is most commonly found and fulfilled.

March 2000
The Ponderosa
South Amboy, NJ

AUTUMN'S GLORY PROMISE
SPRINGS NEW HOPE

R ed's, yellows, greenish gold
with roots below giving life and hold.

F allen leaves leave emptiness
before a blustery sky,

B leeding hearts like barren oaks
darest not cry.

C hilly winter winds torment loves lost
with numbing sorrow tallying cost.

W ith the Master of changing seasons implored
new life may be in season restored.

W ithdrawn awaiting moons
of change above
brings warmth to those
barren in love.

T he tall steely oaks bear the freeze
of winters wailing winds with ease.

F or warmth will overpower soon,
upon an early or mid-spring moon.

R egaining pastures pride ensue
as barren oaks recover anew.

P erhaps within the oaks new life
returns his long lost dove.

I f she can hope and trust again
exploring renewed love.

R. Amato
Morgan, NJ
1999

CALENDAR GIRLS

July is okay most people will say, but June is
gorgeous, perhaps that's what so heats up July,
you know how jealousy can be.
Miss August truly is sublime with wind swept
golden hair in a stately stride. A middle child
always playing the caretaker, Goldie spends herself attempting to cool down July.
September's graces are, however, indispensable,
bringing fruition alas: Lo and behold New England's
forests respond first in celebration.
Decked with bright and fiery colors the
Berkshire Range seems set ablaze.
From October providence falls gracefully in a
full spectrum of colors upon the Mid-Atlantic
states. At the produce markets are displayed the
fruits of her bountiful harvest in crisp Indian
summer days delight. This flamboyant mother
of autumn is as lovely as June, as pleasant
as May.
With all this in mind Miss November tries hard to
please, but people start to talk. She pretends at first
not to hear, but finally she can bear no more

criticism, hence her protests commence with
chilly morning frosts, cold rainy nights, even the
occasional dusting, yet in maturity recounting her
blessings she humbly takes time for Thanksgiving.
Like people of faith December's harshness is
Redeemed by the Christ of her Christmas. Noel
is a hopeful homemaker and cheerful gifter, for
these reasons among others she is perceived strictly
as warm and charming.
So now how do you suppose January will
behave? Jan is exalted as she enters, celebrated
like a new bride, but quickly she is forgotten,
unloved and heaven forbid even criticized,
consequently she grows brutally cold, frigid
indeed.
February like us all at times wishes she were
someone else losing patience and hope no
longer capable of love, yet all of a sudden
in midstream her heart warms and swells,
but courters beware it is only a short season.
Like a bounding lioness March stamps in,
weary of all this fault finding. She enters with
wild roaring winds of retribution, perhaps had
others been kinder, she said, I would not have
been so contrary. Her exit, however, is another
matter as her demeanor becomes almost
lamb like, at times quite amiable.
Sweet April is audacious, daring to press all
extremes from soaking windy tantrums, to warm
brilliantly sunlit days—fragrantly.

All things considered, however, these fertile sisters
of spring sing in three piece harmony an angelic
chorus unto the glorious rebirth of Easter. March,
also called windy broadly scatters autumn's seeds
while Aprils nurturing showers germinate
May's flowers.
May is all dressed up now and gaining on
June as God enters with miracles of new life,
with the covenant rainbow, with blooming forests
and fields and with litters of new pups. Delightfully
adorned May is the envy of artist and you already
know how gorgeous Junie is, but please
don't tell Julie lest she sear us all with
her pretty yet scornful glare.

DEATH'S YEILD IS LIFE ETERNAL

"For God did not appoint us to wrath, but to obtain salvation through our Lord Jesus Christ, who died for us, that whether we wake or sleep, we should live together with Him. Therefore comfort each other and edify one another, just as you also are doing." (1 Thess. 5:9–11)

"O Death, where is your sting?
O Hades, where is your
victory?" (Hos. 13:14)

"For to me, to live is Christ and to die is gain." (Phil. 1:21)

The prophets and apostles have told us a thousand times that dying should be in some mystical way embraced. If, however, one dreads the dying thing then perhaps he thinks it is the last thing, showing his faith in a somewhat compromised position.

"But as many as received Him, to them He gave the right to become children of

God, to those who believe in His name."
(John 1:12)

We may conclude according to the above verses and scores of others, that God is gracious toward us understanding our limitations. True, we have a helper in the Holy Spirit, but we also have a hinderance in his evilness and his horde, some demons some humans. Add to that, we live in a cursed universe under entropies universal law of corruption and decay.

In any event, I have heard and do believe, that often on their death bed people of faith no matter how they balk and panic that as they near the very end, their angels comfort and calm them just before leading them to Paradise, even before the Glorious Throne of our loving Father and before His only begotten Son, the lamb who was slain for our shortcomings. He has promised to lead us forth with all gentleness, for He is our Good Shepherd, our Great King now and forever according to His grace. Amen!

From the Hyson House
Jackson, NJ, Sept. 2005

DELIGHTFUL, WONDEROUS, PECULIAR, MYSTERIOUS

DELIGHTFUL is a harvest moon passing beyond
   the barn and the
autumn trees, while a playful pup startles a pair of
   morning doves.
WONDROUS is the Earth's vine dresser who
   appoints countless
stars in endless space, yet He considers minuscule
   man;
each and every one.
PECULIAR are free willed people whose strivings
   and straining
yield a full field from peril to peace, from respect
   through disdain,
from the marvelous to the mundane.
MYSTERIOUS is His omniscience and fore-
   knowledge, progressively
to us come victories through faith or else loss by
   vanity revealed
as we sojourn here in the consciousness or uncon-
   sciousness of life's
plain and obvious miracle.

"O Lord, our Lord, how excellent is Your name
in all the earth.
Who have set Your glory above the heavens!
When I consider Your heavens the work of Your fingers,
The moon and the stars, which You have ordained,
What is man that You are mindful of him
And the son of man that You visit him?
(Psalm 8:1, 3, 4, NKJV)

SHALLOW DEEP, HOW TO TELL WHAT TO KEEP

Deep inside the Arctic Circle, below the Northern Lights, shallow ice sheets drift aimlessly, scattered by any whispering or wailing winds of change. Like gossip recipients—mislead, unstable. But icebergs that run deep travel according to sure and established currents: like principled subjects of The Great King, routed as destiny's children on course. However, the shallow ice sheets that meander aimlessly and the mammoth bergs in their predestined stride are neither alive nor on trial, but the souls of men are. So what might God be trying to convey to us who would most surely to live? Perhaps, that heaven is where He is and hell is where He is not and that if dumb icebergs can do so purely, so can we most surely. True God is a loving Father and certainly no legalistic tyrant, but He is also justice personified, this is our hope or our fearful dilemma: to be led by love—to be His delight or to be separated from love—through eternal night, or is it simply the obliteration of the soul, which might be far better.

If while living as free and autonomous people we choose to be shallow judges dark and cold, we are to be pitted all the more as we grow old. The principles and warnings are sure and clear; with gossip comes judgment then trouble is near. But peace makers who sow in love deep, forgiving while living forever will reap.

Aurora Borealis where clues of majestic presence lie, where Northern Lights shimmer in dark and blustery sky. How illusive where brightness and blackness mingle, yet only for a time, till rises that "Bright and Morning Star"— Son shining light on all near and far.

Some things need to be discarded others kept, but how just how to choose in obscurity His children sat and wept. You may marvel at illusions, He said, but keep in mind, the Son will show you what to keep and how to find.

Poets at heart know one thing to be true
another's words will never do,
Except for the Logos[42] and this is the clue,
love God and others and for heavens sake
don't forget you.

---

[42] Greek for word another among many names for Jesus.

Ray Amato
Hyson House
Jackson, NJ 2004

LEARNING TO LIVE AMONG DEMONS AND ANGELS

Prodigal Son

Misunderstood, but mostly misunderstanding,
Often hearing, but never quite perceiving,
Half trying, thus rarely prevailing.
Ravaged in chastisement,
Traveling unwieldy among dark shadows,
Raving—beguiled.
Reckless even rebellious,
Still certainly good would to have him;
As surely as he remains unkilled.
Slowly dying while living
Among demons and angels
Who bid my soul.
All we like sheep have gone astray
We have turned everyone to his own way. (Is. 53:6)

Learning To Live Among Demons And Angels

Repentant Son

Understanding at times, at times understood,
Learning, beginning to see
Trying less, trusting more.
Mending upon the shoulders of the Good Shepherd,
Walking in green pastures calmly,
By silent crystalline brooks.
Confident, carefully aware,
Faiths yield is bountiful,
Life's long sojourn best be enlightened.
Learning to live
Among demons and angels
Who bid my soul.

But perhaps I speak too soon and too loud, for
the devils have ears. God help us Amen?
If the Apostle can say it, so can I; "O wretched
man that I am." (Romans 7:24)

ABOUT THE AUTHOR

With sixty years of life experience behind him, Ray has seen many things from the ivy palaces of his early employment to the dingy prison and jails of New Jersey and New York. A father of four with four grandchildren thus far, he has worked in various fields. A golf professional, teaching and playing mostly throughout NJ and Florida in his twenties until marrying when a more stable income became necessary. Following in his dad's footsteps, he became a tractor trailer driver traversing thirty-five states and Canada seeing the most beautiful landscapes from the seacoast to the mountain ranges, meeting many different people of various cultures and dialects. Not a reader yet at this stage in his life, he would fill those lonely miles listening to the Bible on cassette tapes, not realizing he was being groomed as an evangelistic writer. During the road years, delight mixes with disappointment and sorrows due to two broken families and a number of incarcerations due to the revisitation of some old bad habits of his youth. God was there through it all, however teaching an encouraging sometimes blessing sometimes chastising. When God finally saw fit to make a writer out of the writer, He did it in unique fashion. Upon entering the first county jail cell of his longest and final prison stay, he noticed that it was unoccupied, except for the leather-bound New King James Version of the Bible, which to this day is still his favorite. And if you can believe, the next most important book for a Bible teacher, a brand-new *Strong's Concise Concordance* of the Bible still in cellophane wrap. Now this all seemed far too unlikely to be a coincidence. (Almost instantly imbued with enthusiasm and a rush of energy, earnest prayer ensued, yielding clear ideas even enlightenment.) With much prayer and study, the writing began to flow. The contents of this book of short stories, theological essays, and poetry is in part the product of that time.